T0368258

365 DAILY
Inspirational Thoughts
AND PRAYER JOURNAL

JOEY EDWARDS

WESTBOW
PRESS®
A DIVISION OF THOMAS NELSON
& ZONDERVAN

WestBow Press books may be ordered through booksellers or by contacting:

WestBow Press
A Division of Thomas Nelson & Zondervan
1663 Liberty Drive
Bloomington, IN 47403
www.westbowpress.com
1 (866) 928-1240

ISBN: 978-1-9736-9815-9 (sc)
ISBN: 978-1-9736-9816-6 (hc)
ISBN: 978-1-9736-9814-2 (e)

Library of Congress Control Number: 2020913091

Print information available on the last page.

WestBow Press rev. date: 07/30/2020

DEDICATION

This collection of daily inspirational thoughts is dedicated to my family (Leanne, Drew, Will, Zach and Gavin, Tyler and Katelyn, and Kaylee and Carter), church family (Court Avenue Cumberland Presbyterian Church, Selmer TN), former and current students (LeMoyne-Owen College, Bethel University), high school classmates (Westview High School, Martin TN Class of 78), and other friends and family who have received these daily inspirations for some time by email and text; some since 2008. It is amazing how God continues to work through these to encourage and inspire many each day.

FOREWORD

"For the past 40+ years, I have known Joey Edwards as we graduated high school together. We lost touch for a long time before reunions and Facebook and we have been blessed to be reconnected now for several years. My first 'Inspirational Thought' was received October 21, 2011. I have read each and every one through the years and I archive them to reference when needed. They have been such a blessing to me. I have 2,874 messages I can refer to at any time to provide me hope, comfort, and strength in a world right now that seems to be drifting away. I have shared many of these messages with those I work with, those going through tough times, and they have reached people most will never know. Below is the first 'Inspirational Thought' I ever received. Just reading this now fills my heart with love for Jesus, as it speaks to the fact that when you **love God,** you'll naturally **love people**, which are the two greatest commandments."

October 21, 2011

When you have learned to love God better than everyone else, your love for everyone else will be better.

"Love the Lord your God with all your heart, with all your soul, and with all your mind." Matthew 22:37 NIV

John Mark Johnson, Dresden TN

PREFACE

This collection of daily inspirational thoughts are a few of many that have accumulated over several years of daily quiet time devotions that have been shared with many on a daily basis. Although many are original inspired thoughts, some, whether partially or in whole, have come from the compiler's study and reading of other pastors and/or devotional books. Many have been written down from sources that included old inspirational calendars, sermon notes, professor lectures at Memphis Theological Seminary, etc. Favorites of the compiler include Charles Stanley, Tony Evans, Charles Swindoll, Adrian Rodgers, Max Lucado, Zig Ziglar, Toby Mac, David Jeremiah, Henry Blackaby, and many others. Each daily thought is for the inspiration of the reader to draw closer to God and to be inspired to live that day fulfilling their purpose for Christ. The scriptures at the bottom of each page will cover the entire Bible in 365 days. The goal is to focus on today, one day at a time.

It is my prayer that God will speak to you or someone you know through many of these devotions, that you will grow closer to Him through daily quiet time and the compiling of your prayer journal, and that you will be able to read through the Bible in 365 days (or more).

DAY 1

Just when you think the drought is inevitable and the well will run dry, God sends the rain.

> *"The Lord will guide you always; He will satisfy your needs in a sun-scorched land...you will be like a well-watered garden, like a spring whose waters never fail."*
> *Isaiah 58:11 KJV*

PRAYER LIST	TO DO LIST
1. _____	1. _____
2. _____	2. _____
3. _____	3. _____
4. _____	4. _____
5. _____	5. _____
6. _____	6. _____
7. _____	7. _____

Prayer journal notes:

Genesis 1-3; Matthew 1

_____
_____
_____
_____
_____
_____
_____
_____

DAY 2

When you are humble and obedient, you cannot outrun the good things of God.
Humility + Obedience = Blessings

> *"If you keep My commands, you will remain in My love."*
> *John 15:10 NIV*

PRAYER LIST	TO DO LIST
1. _____	1. _____
2. _____	2. _____
3. _____	3. _____
4. _____	4. _____
5. _____	5. _____
6. _____	6. _____
7. _____	7. _____

Prayer journal notes:

Genesis 4-6; Matthew 2

_____

_____

_____

_____

_____

_____

_____

_____

_____

DAY 3

~∽

Be a preacher today. Preach Christ at all times; use words if necessary!

> *"Woe to me if I do not preach the gospel."*
> *1 Corinthians 9:16 NIV*

PRAYER LIST	TO DO LIST
1. _____	1. _____
2. _____	2. _____
3. _____	3. _____
4. _____	4. _____
5. _____	5. _____
6. _____	6. _____
7. _____	7. _____

Prayer journal notes:

Genesis 7-9; Matthew 3

_____

_____

_____

_____

_____

_____

_____

_____

_____

_____

_____

DAY 4

~⦿~

Someone in your path today needs your love!

> *"…all men will know you are My disciples if you love one another."*
>
> *John 13:34 NIV*

PRAYER LIST	TO DO LIST
1. _____	1. _____
2. _____	2. _____
3. _____	3. _____
4. _____	4. _____
5. _____	5. _____
6. _____	6. _____
7. _____	7. _____

Prayer journal notes:

Genesis 10-12; Matthew 4

_____

_____

_____

_____

_____

_____

_____

_____

_____

_____

_____

DAY 5

If you just take a look around, you will be reminded that our God is an awesome God!

> "...for the Lord your God, who is among you, is a great and awesome God."
>
> Deuteronomy 7:21 NIV

PRAYER LIST	TO DO LIST
1. _____	1. _____
2. _____	2. _____
3. _____	3. _____
4. _____	4. _____
5. _____	5. _____
6. _____	6. _____
7. _____	7. _____

Prayer journal notes:

Genesis 13-15; Matthew 5:1-20

_____

_____

_____

_____

_____

_____

_____

_____

_____

_____

DAY 6

❦

You are a representative of God in all that you do; at home, at work, at school, at the ball game, at the grocery store, at the doctor's office. Represent well!

> *"We are ambassadors for Christ..."*
> *2 Corinthians 5:20 KJV*

PRAYER LIST	TO DO LIST
1. _____	1. _____
2. _____	2. _____
3. _____	3. _____
4. _____	4. _____
5. _____	5. _____
6. _____	6. _____
7. _____	7. _____

Prayer journal notes:

Genesis 16-17; Matthew 5:21-48

_____

_____

_____

_____

_____

_____

_____

_____

_____

DAY 7

~⌒⌒

When troubles come, you can allow them to make you bitter, or better.

"They cried to the Lord in their trouble, and He saved them from their distress."

Psalm 107:13 NIV

PRAYER LIST	TO DO LIST
1. _____	1. _____
2. _____	2. _____
3. _____	3. _____
4. _____	4. _____
5. _____	5. _____
6. _____	6. _____
7. _____	7. _____

Prayer journal notes:

Genesis 18-19; Matthew 6:1-15

_____

_____

_____

_____

_____

_____

_____

_____

_____

DAY 8

Accepting anything other than God's will is settling for second best.

"Teach me to do Your will, for You are my God."
Psalm 143:10 NIV

PRAYER LIST	TO DO LIST
1. _____	1. _____
2. _____	2. _____
3. _____	3. _____
4. _____	4. _____
5. _____	5. _____
6. _____	6. _____
7. _____	7. _____

Prayer journal notes:

Genesis 20-22; Matthew 6:16-34

_____

_____

_____

_____

_____

_____

_____

_____

_____

_____

_____

DAY 9

∽◯

If you are in an area of confusion that refuses to clear up, you need to find another area. God does not dwell in confusion.

"God is not the author of confusion, but of peace"
1 Corinthians 14:33 NKJV

PRAYER LIST	TO DO LIST
1. _____	1. _____
2. _____	2. _____
3. _____	3. _____
4. _____	4. _____
5. _____	5. _____
6. _____	6. _____
7. _____	7. _____

Prayer journal notes:

Genesis 23-24; Matthew 7

_____
_____
_____
_____
_____
_____
_____
_____
_____
_____
_____

DAY 10

If faith can move mountains, and love is greater than faith, just imagine what love can do.

> *"And now these three remain: faith, hope, and love. And the greatest of these is love."*
>
> *1 Corinthians 13:13 NIV*

PRAYER LIST	TO DO LIST
1. _____	1. _____
2. _____	2. _____
3. _____	3. _____
4. _____	4. _____
5. _____	5. _____
6. _____	6. _____
7. _____	7. _____

Prayer journal notes:

Genesis 25-26; Matthew 8:1-17

_____

_____

_____

_____

_____

_____

_____

_____

_____

DAY 11

If you follow Jesus, expect your plans to be interrupted frequently. The agenda belongs to the Master, not the servant.

"And I will show you the most excellent way."

1 Corinthians 12:31 NIV

PRAYER LIST	TO DO LIST
1. _____	1. _____
2. _____	2. _____
3. _____	3. _____
4. _____	4. _____
5. _____	5. _____
6. _____	6. _____
7. _____	7. _____

Prayer journal notes:

Genesis 27-28; Matthew 8:18-34

_____
_____
_____
_____
_____
_____
_____
_____
_____

DAY 12

Even in our weakest moments, we stand strong because the strength we rely on is not that of our own.

> *"The Lord is my strength and my shield; my heart trusts in Him and I am helped."*
>
> *Psalm 28:7 NIV*

PRAYER LIST	TO DO LIST
1. _____	1. _____
2. _____	2. _____
3. _____	3. _____
4. _____	4. _____
5. _____	5. _____
6. _____	6. _____
7. _____	7. _____

Prayer journal notes:

Genesis 29-30; Matthew 9:1-17

_____

_____

_____

_____

_____

_____

_____

_____

_____

_____

DAY 13

When we are given something we don't deserve, that is grace. When we are given something we don't deserve that lasts for eternity; that is amazing grace.

"Surely you have heard about the administration of God's grace..."

Ephesians 3:2 NIV

PRAYER LIST	TO DO LIST
1. _____	1. _____
2. _____	2. _____
3. _____	3. _____
4. _____	4. _____
5. _____	5. _____
6. _____	6. _____
7. _____	7. _____

Prayer journal notes:

Genesis 31-32; Matthew 9:18-38

_____
_____
_____
_____
_____
_____
_____
_____
_____

DAY 14

We must not let "The Great Commission" from Jesus turn into "The Great Omission," or "The Limited Agreement For Those Who Show Up at My Church Who Look Like Me."

"Therefore go and make disciples of all nations, baptizing them in the name of the Father and of the Son and of the Holy Spirit, and teaching them to obey everything I have commanded you."

Matthew 28:19-20 NIV

PRAYER LIST	TO DO LIST
1. _____	1. _____
2. _____	2. _____
3. _____	3. _____
4. _____	4. _____
5. _____	5. _____
6. _____	6. _____
7. _____	7. _____

Prayer journal notes:

Genesis 33-35; Matthew 10:1-20

_____
_____
_____
_____
_____
_____
_____

DAY 15

We can pray, trusting that God not just hears our words, but our heart; and He answers by giving us more than what we ask for, but instead what's best for us.

"He answered their prayers because they trusted in Him."
1 Chronicles 5:20 NIV

PRAYER LIST	TO DO LIST
1. _____	1. _____
2. _____	2. _____
3. _____	3. _____
4. _____	4. _____
5. _____	5. _____
6. _____	6. _____
7. _____	7. _____

Prayer journal notes:

Genesis 36-38; Matthew 10:21-42

_____
_____
_____
_____
_____
_____
_____
_____
_____

DAY 16

Sometimes, to get where we need to be, we have to give up something. It may be a bad habit, a hobby that takes up too much of our time, or someone who is a bad influence. Short term sacrifices for long-term gain.
It will be worth it.

"Throwing his cloak aside he came to Jesus...immediately he received his sight and followed Him."

Mark 10:50-52 NIV

PRAYER LIST	TO DO LIST
1. _____	1. _____
2. _____	2. _____
3. _____	3. _____
4. _____	4. _____
5. _____	5. _____
6. _____	6. _____
7. _____	7. _____

Prayer journal notes:

Genesis 39-40; Matthew 11

_____

_____

_____

_____

_____

_____

_____

DAY 17

Today is one of the best days ever, for you to have one of your best days ever.

> *"This is the day that the Lord has made; I will rejoice and be glad in it."*
>
> Psalm 118:24 NKJV

PRAYER LIST	TO DO LIST
1. _____	1. _____
2. _____	2. _____
3. _____	3. _____
4. _____	4. _____
5. _____	5. _____
6. _____	6. _____
7. _____	7. _____

Prayer journal notes:

Genesis 41-42; Matthew 12:1-23

_____
_____
_____
_____
_____
_____
_____
_____
_____

DAY 18

A bumper sticker says, "God is my Co-Pilot." Better to be co-pilot than not in the car. But you need to swap seats. God should be THE pilot. And He doesn't need a backseat driver.

"From the ends of the earth I call to You...lead me to the rock that is higher than I."

Psalm 61:2 NIV

PRAYER LIST	TO DO LIST
1. _____	1. _____
2. _____	2. _____
3. _____	3. _____
4. _____	4. _____
5. _____	5. _____
6. _____	6. _____
7. _____	7. _____

Prayer journal notes:

Genesis 43-45; Matthew 12:24-50

_____
_____
_____
_____
_____
_____
_____
_____

DAY 19

Be careful what you pray for, because you just might get it, and then regret it. Always pray for God's will to be done, not yours. Then there are no regrets because you know it's what's best for you.

"Jesus said, 'You don't know what you are asking.'"
Mark 10:38 NIV

PRAYER LIST	TO DO LIST
1. _____	1. _____
2. _____	2. _____
3. _____	3. _____
4. _____	4. _____
5. _____	5. _____
6. _____	6. _____
7. _____	7. _____

Prayer journal notes:

Genesis 46-48; Matthew 13:1-30

_____
_____
_____
_____
_____
_____
_____
_____

DAY 20

In prison for a crime he didn't commit, Joseph remained positive, faithful, and committed. Life may be unfair at times, but stay positive and faithful. God always has a plan.

> *"Joseph's master took him and put him in prison...when two full years had past...Pharaoh said to Joseph, 'I put you in charge of the whole land of Egypt.'"*
> Genesis 39:20-41 NIV

PRAYER LIST	TO DO LIST
1. _____	1. _____
2. _____	2. _____
3. _____	3. _____
4. _____	4. _____
5. _____	5. _____
6. _____	6. _____
7. _____	7. _____

Prayer journal notes:

Genesis 49-50; Matthew 13:31-58

_____
_____
_____
_____
_____
_____
_____
_____
_____

DAY 21

May your words and actions to others today be proof to them that God is alive and loves them.

"Let your light shine before men, that they may see your good deeds and praise your Father in heaven."
Matthew 5:16 NIV

PRAYER LIST	TO DO LIST
1. _____	1. _____
2. _____	2. _____
3. _____	3. _____
4. _____	4. _____
5. _____	5. _____
6. _____	6. _____
7. _____	7. _____

Prayer journal notes:

Exodus 1-3; Matthew 14:1-21

_____
_____
_____
_____
_____
_____
_____
_____
_____

DAY 22

Your heart can only pretend to be where your treasure is not at. If you want a change of heart, your treasure must change.

"For where your treasure is, there you heart will be also."
Luke 12:34 NIV

PRAYER LIST	TO DO LIST
1. _____	1. _____
2. _____	2. _____
3. _____	3. _____
4. _____	4. _____
5. _____	5. _____
6. _____	6. _____
7. _____	7. _____

Prayer journal notes:

Exodus 4-6; Matthew 14:22-36

_____
_____
_____
_____
_____
_____
_____
_____
_____
_____
_____

DAY 23

Every small step of faith equals a large step of growth. Keep stepping.

> *"Now faith is being sure of what we hope for and certain of what we do not see."*
>
> *Hebrews 11:1 NIV*

PRAYER LIST	TO DO LIST
1. _____	1. _____
2. _____	2. _____
3. _____	3. _____
4. _____	4. _____
5. _____	5. _____
6. _____	6. _____
7. _____	7. _____

Prayer journal notes:

Exodus 7-8; Matthew 15:1-20

_____

_____

_____

_____

_____

_____

_____

_____

DAY 24

Don't major in minor things. Stay focused. You cannot have a clear vision as long as you are in the weeds.

"Let us throw off everything that hinders and the sin that so easily entangles…"

Hebrews 12:1 NIV

PRAYER LIST	TO DO LIST
1. _____	1. _____
2. _____	2. _____
3. _____	3. _____
4. _____	4. _____
5. _____	5. _____
6. _____	6. _____
7. _____	7. _____

Prayer journal notes:

Exodus 9-11; Matthew 15:21-39

_____

_____

_____

_____

_____

_____

_____

_____

_____

DAY 25

365 times in the Bible we are told not to fear. That's one for each day of the year. That includes today. So whatever you are facing today, God's got you covered.

"So do not fear for I am with you; do not be dismayed, for I am your God."

Isaiah 41:10 NIV

PRAYER LIST	TO DO LIST
1. _____	1. _____
2. _____	2. _____
3. _____	3. _____
4. _____	4. _____
5. _____	5. _____
6. _____	6. _____
7. _____	7. _____

Prayer journal notes:

Exodus 12-13; Matthew 16

_____
_____
_____
_____
_____
_____
_____
_____

DAY 26

Crossing the Jordan River at flood stage seemed impossible. But just follow God's lead and leave the details to Him.

"The water from upstream stopped flowing. It piled up in a heap…until the whole nation had completed the crossing on dry ground."

Joshua 3:16-17 NIV

PRAYER LIST	TO DO LIST
1. _____	1. _____
2. _____	2. _____
3. _____	3. _____
4. _____	4. _____
5. _____	5. _____
6. _____	6. _____
7. _____	7. _____

Prayer journal notes:

Exodus 14-15; Matthew 17

_____

_____

_____

_____

_____

_____

_____

_____

DAY 27

⌒⌒

People remember those who make a positive difference in their lives. Be remembered.

"Wherever this gospel is preached throughout the world, what she has done will also be told in memory of her."
Matthew 25:13 NIV

PRAYER LIST	TO DO LIST
1. _____	1. _____
2. _____	2. _____
3. _____	3. _____
4. _____	4. _____
5. _____	5. _____
6. _____	6. _____
7. _____	7. _____

Prayer journal notes:

Exodus 16-18; Matthew 18:1-20

_____
_____
_____
_____
_____
_____
_____
_____
_____
_____

DAY 28

Sometimes God leads us to battle so we can see His power in victory and He will be glorified.

> *"And I will harden Pharaoh's heart and he will pursue them. But I will gain glory for Myself through Pharaoh and all his army...the Egyptians will know that I am the Lord."*
>
> *Exodus 14:17-18 NIV*

PRAYER LIST	TO DO LIST
1. _____	1. _____
2. _____	2. _____
3. _____	3. _____
4. _____	4. _____
5. _____	5. _____
6. _____	6. _____
7. _____	7. _____

Prayer journal notes:

Exodus 19-20; Matthew 18:21-35

_____
_____
_____
_____
_____
_____
_____
_____

DAY 29

You are encouraged when you encourage someone. Words of encouragement can completely change someone's day. Go out of your way to encourage someone today.

"Therefore encourage one another and build each other up."
1 Thessalonians 5:11 NIV

PRAYER LIST	TO DO LIST
1. _____	1. _____
2. _____	2. _____
3. _____	3. _____
4. _____	4. _____
5. _____	5. _____
6. _____	6. _____
7. _____	7. _____

Prayer journal notes:

Exodus 21-22; Matthew 19

_____

_____

_____

_____

_____

_____

_____

_____

_____

DAY 30

No matter what you've been through, no matter the bumps, bruises or scars; you are loved. God loves you more than you can comprehend, and nothing can change that.

"But God demonstrates His own love toward us, in that while we were still sinners, Christ died for us."

Romans 5:8 NKJV

PRAYER LIST	TO DO LIST
1. _____	1. _____
2. _____	2. _____
3. _____	3. _____
4. _____	4. _____
5. _____	5. _____
6. _____	6. _____
7. _____	7. _____

Prayer journal notes:

Exodus 23-24; Matthew 20:1-16

_____

_____

_____

_____

_____

_____

_____

_____

DAY 31

When our faithfulness waivers, we can be comforted in knowing that God's faithfulness does not.

"Let us hold unswervingly to the hope we profess, for He who promised is faithful."

Hebrews 10:23 NIV

PRAYER LIST	TO DO LIST
1. _____	1. _____
2. _____	2. _____
3. _____	3. _____
4. _____	4. _____
5. _____	5. _____
6. _____	6. _____
7. _____	7. _____

Prayer journal notes:

Exodus 25-26; Matthew 20:17-34

_____

_____

_____

_____

_____

_____

_____

_____

_____

_____

DAY 32

God is all-powerful and can do anything. He spoke the earth into existence, but He will not do for us what He expects us to do. He will lead us and show us what needs to be done, but God doesn't do lazy.

> *"Make this tabernacle and all its furnishings exactly like the pattern I will show you."*
>
> Exodus 25:9 NIV

PRAYER LIST	TO DO LIST
1. _____	1. _____
2. _____	2. _____
3. _____	3. _____
4. _____	4. _____
5. _____	5. _____
6. _____	6. _____
7. _____	7. _____

Prayer journal notes:

Exodus 27-28; Matthew 21:1-22

_____
_____
_____
_____
_____
_____
_____
_____
_____

DAY 33

❦

God expects for us to be fruit-bearers. We each have a chance
to do so today. Let us not miss that chance.

> *"Leave it alone for one more year, and I'll dig around
> it and fertilize it. If it bears fruit next year, fine! If not,
> then cut it down."*
>
> *Luke 13:8-9 NIV*

PRAYER LIST	TO DO LIST
1. _____	1. _____
2. _____	2. _____
3. _____	3. _____
4. _____	4. _____
5. _____	5. _____
6. _____	6. _____
7. _____	7. _____

Prayer journal notes:

Exodus 29-30; Matthew 21:23-46

_____

_____

_____

_____

_____

_____

_____

_____

DAY 34

Communication is key in any relationship that is strong, including our relationship with God. If you are too busy to pray, you are too busy.

"...so that nothing will hinder your prayers."
1 Peter 3:7 NIV

PRAYER LIST	TO DO LIST
1. _____	1. _____
2. _____	2. _____
3. _____	3. _____
4. _____	4. _____
5. _____	5. _____
6. _____	6. _____
7. _____	7. _____

Prayer journal notes:

Exodus 31-33; Matthew 22:1-22

_____

_____

_____

_____

_____

_____

_____

_____

_____

DAY 35

Allow your enjoyment of God and the excitement of abundant life to spill over in every aspect of your day today.

> *"So I commend the enjoyment of life. . .joy will accompany him in his work all the days of the life God has given him under the sun."*
>
> *Ecclesiastes 8:15 NIV*

PRAYER LIST	TO DO LIST
1. _____	1. _____
2. _____	2. _____
3. _____	3. _____
4. _____	4. _____
5. _____	5. _____
6. _____	6. _____
7. _____	7. _____

Prayer journal notes:

Exodus 34-35; Matthew 22:23-46

_____
_____
_____
_____
_____
_____
_____
_____

DAY 36

Sometimes life seems like running an obstacle course in the dark. But then the light comes on.

"Your Word is a lamp to my feet and a light for my path."
Psalm 119:105 NIV

PRAYER LIST	TO DO LIST
1. _____	1. _____
2. _____	2. _____
3. _____	3. _____
4. _____	4. _____
5. _____	5. _____
6. _____	6. _____
7. _____	7. _____

Prayer journal notes:

Exodus 36-38; Matthew 23:1-22

_____
_____
_____
_____
_____
_____
_____
_____
_____
_____
_____

DAY 37

We don't have to worry about what the future holds when we know the One who holds the future.

"He is before all things, and in Him all things hold together."
Colossians 1:17 NIV

PRAYER LIST	TO DO LIST
1. _____	1. _____
2. _____	2. _____
3. _____	3. _____
4. _____	4. _____
5. _____	5. _____
6. _____	6. _____
7. _____	7. _____

Prayer journal notes:

Exodus 39-40; Matthew 23:23-39

_____
_____
_____
_____
_____
_____
_____
_____
_____
_____
_____

DAY 38

Don't be so busy that you fail to see God's daily wonders and blessings around you.

"Stop and consider God's wonders..."

Job 37:14 NIV

PRAYER LIST	TO DO LIST
1. _____	1. _____
2. _____	2. _____
3. _____	3. _____
4. _____	4. _____
5. _____	5. _____
6. _____	6. _____
7. _____	7. _____

Prayer journal notes:

Leviticus 1-3; Matthew 24:1-28

_____

_____

_____

_____

_____

_____

_____

_____

_____

_____

DAY 39

Loving you makes God happy. You are one of His favorites. If He had a refrigerator, your picture would be on the front of it.

"The Lord your God is with you...He takes great delight in you...He will rejoice over you with singing."
Zephaniah 3:17 NIV

PRAYER LIST	TO DO LIST
1. _____	1. _____
2. _____	2. _____
3. _____	3. _____
4. _____	4. _____
5. _____	5. _____
6. _____	6. _____
7. _____	7. _____

Prayer journal notes:

Leviticus 4-5; Matthew 24:29-51

_____
_____
_____
_____
_____
_____
_____
_____
_____
_____

DAY 40

Worship is an everyday experience for those walking close with God. May your worship today make God smile!

"The Lord is pleased with those who worship Him and trust His love."

Psalm 147:11 CEV

PRAYER LIST	TO DO LIST
1. _____	1. _____
2. _____	2. _____
3. _____	3. _____
4. _____	4. _____
5. _____	5. _____
6. _____	6. _____
7. _____	7. _____

Prayer journal notes:

Leviticus 6-7; Matthew 25:1-30

_____

_____

_____

_____

_____

_____

_____

_____

_____

_____

DAY 41

There is no reason to worry about daily bread when your Father owns the bakery.

"It is the bread the Lord has given you to eat...each one gathered as much as he needed."

Exodus 16:15,18 NIV

PRAYER LIST	TO DO LIST
1. _____	1. _____
2. _____	2. _____
3. _____	3. _____
4. _____	4. _____
5. _____	5. _____
6. _____	6. _____
7. _____	7. _____

Prayer journal notes:

Leviticus 8-10; Matthew 25:31-46

_____
_____
_____
_____
_____
_____
_____
_____
_____

DAY 42

The difference between ordinary and extra-ordinary is that little something extra.

> *"Whatever your hand finds to do, do it with all your might."*
>
> Ecclesiastes 9:10 NIV

PRAYER LIST	TO DO LIST
1. _____	1. _____
2. _____	2. _____
3. _____	3. _____
4. _____	4. _____
5. _____	5. _____
6. _____	6. _____
7. _____	7. _____

Prayer journal notes:

Leviticus 11-12; Matthew 26:1-25

_____

_____

_____

_____

_____

_____

_____

_____

_____

DAY 43

୧୦

God loves us and is always there, but will intervene in our affairs by invitation only.

> *"Here I am. I stand at the door and knock. If anyone hears My voice and opens the door, I will come in."*
>
> *Revelation 3:20 NIV*

PRAYER LIST	TO DO LIST
1. _____	1. _____
2. _____	2. _____
3. _____	3. _____
4. _____	4. _____
5. _____	5. _____
6. _____	6. _____
7. _____	7. _____

Prayer journal notes:

Leviticus 13; Matthew 26:26-50

_____

_____

_____

_____

_____

_____

_____

_____

DAY 44

When things go wrong, don't go wrong with them.

> *"Do not set foot on the path of the wicked or walk in the way of evil men."*
>
> Proverbs 4:14 NIV

PRAYER LIST	TO DO LIST
1. _____	1. _____
2. _____	2. _____
3. _____	3. _____
4. _____	4. _____
5. _____	5. _____
6. _____	6. _____
7. _____	7. _____

Prayer journal notes:

Leviticus 14; Matthew 26:51-71

_____
_____
_____
_____
_____
_____
_____
_____
_____
_____
_____

DAY 45

Make it happen. A field will never get plowed just by turning it over in your mind.

"The harvest is plentiful, but the workers are few."
Matthew 9:37 NIV

PRAYER LIST	TO DO LIST
1. _____	1. _____
2. _____	2. _____
3. _____	3. _____
4. _____	4. _____
5. _____	5. _____
6. _____	6. _____
7. _____	7. _____

Prayer journal notes:

Leviticus 15-16; Matthew 27:1-26

_____

_____

_____

_____

_____

_____

_____

_____

_____

_____

_____

DAY 46

Nothing ventured, nothing gained. You will never walk on the water if you don't get out of the boat.

> *"Then Peter got down out of the boat, walked on the water and came toward Jesus."*
>
> *Matthew 14:29 NIV*

PRAYER LIST	TO DO LIST
1. _____	1. _____
2. _____	2. _____
3. _____	3. _____
4. _____	4. _____
5. _____	5. _____
6. _____	6. _____
7. _____	7. _____

Prayer journal notes:

Leviticus 17-18; Matthew 27:27-50

_____

_____

_____

_____

_____

_____

_____

_____

_____

_____

DAY 47

〰️

Those who deserve love the least need it the most. Love and pray for your enemies until they are no longer your enemies.

"Love your enemies and pray for those who persecute you."
Matthew 5:44 NIV

PRAYER LIST	TO DO LIST
1. _____	1. _____
2. _____	2. _____
3. _____	3. _____
4. _____	4. _____
5. _____	5. _____
6. _____	6. _____
7. _____	7. _____

Prayer journal notes:

Leviticus 19-20; Matthew 27:51-66

_____

_____

_____

_____

_____

_____

_____

_____

_____

_____

DAY 48

Many times you must receive correction from God before you receive direction from God.

> *"Do not make light of the Lord's discipline...because the Lord disciplines those He loves."*
>
> Hebrews 12:5-6 NIV

PRAYER LIST	TO DO LIST
1. _____	1. _____
2. _____	2. _____
3. _____	3. _____
4. _____	4. _____
5. _____	5. _____
6. _____	6. _____
7. _____	7. _____

Prayer journal notes:

Leviticus 21-22; Matthew 28

_____

_____

_____

_____

_____

_____

_____

_____

_____

DAY 49

Do everything, no matter how insignificant or small it seems, to the very best of your ability. It's the little things in life that determine the big things.

"Well done, good and faithful servant! You have been faithful with a few things; I will put you in charge of many things."

Matthew 25:23 NIV

PRAYER LIST	TO DO LIST
1. _____	1. _____
2. _____	2. _____
3. _____	3. _____
4. _____	4. _____
5. _____	5. _____
6. _____	6. _____
7. _____	7. _____

Prayer journal notes:

Leviticus 23-24; Mark 1:1-22

_____

_____

_____

_____

_____

_____

_____

_____

DAY 50

Pray about everything, no matter how small.
Any problem too small to pray about is too small to worry about.

"Casting all your care upon Him, for He cares for you."
1 Peter 5:7 NKJV

PRAYER LIST	TO DO LIST
1. _____	1. _____
2. _____	2. _____
3. _____	3. _____
4. _____	4. _____
5. _____	5. _____
6. _____	6. _____
7. _____	7. _____

Prayer journal notes:

Leviticus 25; Mark 1:23-45

_____
_____
_____
_____
_____
_____
_____
_____
_____
_____

DAY 51

When walking and talking with God become a priority, abundant life becomes a lifestyle.

> *"Blessed are those who have learned to acclaim You, who walk in the light of your presence, O Lord."*
>
> *Psalm 89:15 NIV*

PRAYER LIST	TO DO LIST
1. _____	1. _____
2. _____	2. _____
3. _____	3. _____
4. _____	4. _____
5. _____	5. _____
6. _____	6. _____
7. _____	7. _____

Prayer journal notes:

Leviticus 26-27; Mark 2

_____

_____

_____

_____

_____

_____

_____

_____

_____

DAY 52

The secret of accomplishing a dreaded task is to not let what you are doing get to you before you get to it.

"Commit to the Lord whatever you do and your plans will succeed."

Proverbs 16:3 NIV

PRAYER LIST	TO DO LIST
1. _____	1. _____
2. _____	2. _____
3. _____	3. _____
4. _____	4. _____
5. _____	5. _____
6. _____	6. _____
7. _____	7. _____

Prayer journal notes:

Numbers 1-2; Mark 3:1-19

_____

_____

_____

_____

_____

_____

_____

_____

_____

DAY 53

~⌒~

Make every day count. When you finish the race of this life here on earth, have no regrets.

"I press on toward the goal to win the prize for which God has called me heavenward in Christ Jesus."

Philippians 3:13-14 NIV

PRAYER LIST	TO DO LIST
1. _____	1. _____
2. _____	2. _____
3. _____	3. _____
4. _____	4. _____
5. _____	5. _____
6. _____	6. _____
7. _____	7. _____

Prayer journal notes:

Numbers 3-4; Mark 3:20-35

_____
_____
_____
_____
_____
_____
_____
_____
_____

DAY 54

Be careful with whom you run with. Your friends are like buttons on an elevator. They will either take you up or take you down.

> *"He who walks with the wise grows wise, but a companion of fools suffers harm."*
>
> *Proverbs 13:20 NIV*

PRAYER LIST	TO DO LIST
1. _____	1. _____
2. _____	2. _____
3. _____	3. _____
4. _____	4. _____
5. _____	5. _____
6. _____	6. _____
7. _____	7. _____

Prayer journal notes:

Numbers 5-6; Mark 4:1-20

_____
_____
_____
_____
_____
_____
_____
_____

DAY 55

The words "mediocre" and "lazy" are inconsistent with the meaning of Christian. There was not a lazy bone in Jesus' body.

> *"If a man is lazy, the rafters sag; if his hands are idle, the house leaks."*
>
> *Ecclesiastes 10:18 NIV*

PRAYER LIST	TO DO LIST
1. _____	1. _____
2. _____	2. _____
3. _____	3. _____
4. _____	4. _____
5. _____	5. _____
6. _____	6. _____
7. _____	7. _____

Prayer journal notes:

Numbers 7-8; Mark 4:21-41

_____

_____

_____

_____

_____

_____

_____

_____

DAY 56

When someone does you wrong, forgiving them is not for them as much as it is for you.

> *"If you forgive men when they sin against you, your heavenly Father will also forgive you."*
>
> Matthew 6:14 NIV

PRAYER LIST	TO DO LIST
1. _____	1. _____
2. _____	2. _____
3. _____	3. _____
4. _____	4. _____
5. _____	5. _____
6. _____	6. _____
7. _____	7. _____

Prayer journal notes:

Numbers 9-11; Mark 5:1-20

_____

_____

_____

_____

_____

_____

_____

_____

_____

_____

DAY 57

Why continue to struggle on your own? You can accomplish more in one hour with God than you can in a lifetime without Him.

"With God, all things are possible."

Matthew 19:26 NIV

PRAYER LIST	TO DO LIST
1. _____	1. _____
2. _____	2. _____
3. _____	3. _____
4. _____	4. _____
5. _____	5. _____
6. _____	6. _____
7. _____	7. _____

Prayer journal notes:

Numbers 12-14; Mark 5:21-43

_____

_____

_____

_____

_____

_____

_____

_____

_____

DAY 58

Prayer is always recommended. Sometimes it is required.

> *"There is no way to get rid of this kind of demon except by prayer."*
>
> *Mark 9:29 NIV*

PRAYER LIST	TO DO LIST
1. _____	1. _____
2. _____	2. _____
3. _____	3. _____
4. _____	4. _____
5. _____	5. _____
6. _____	6. _____
7. _____	7. _____

Prayer journal notes:

Numbers 15-16; Mark 6:1-29

_____

_____

_____

_____

_____

_____

_____

_____

_____

_____

_____

DAY 59

When God blesses you financially, He expects to raise your standard of giving, not just your standard of living.

"Freely you have received, freely give."

Matthew 10:8 NIV

PRAYER LIST	TO DO LIST
1. _____	1. _____
2. _____	2. _____
3. _____	3. _____
4. _____	4. _____
5. _____	5. _____
6. _____	6. _____
7. _____	7. _____

Prayer journal notes:

Numbers 17-19; Mark 6:30-56

_____
_____
_____
_____
_____
_____
_____
_____
_____
_____
_____

DAY 60

Seize the day. Redeem the "now" moments of your life. Stop and smell the roses today. Before you know it, they will no longer be in bloom.

> *"Redeeming the time, because the days are evil."*
> *Ephesians 5:16 NKJV*

PRAYER LIST	TO DO LIST
1. _____	1. _____
2. _____	2. _____
3. _____	3. _____
4. _____	4. _____
5. _____	5. _____
6. _____	6. _____
7. _____	7. _____

Prayer journal notes:

Numbers 20-22; Mark 7:1-13

_____

_____

_____

_____

_____

_____

_____

_____

_____

DAY 61

∽⌒◯

There continues to be a simple pattern that has occurred throughout history. Those who walk in God's ways and follow His commands are blessed.

> *"Observe what the Lord your God requires: walk in His ways, and keep His decrees and commands...so that you may prosper in all you do and wherever you go."*
>
> *2 Kings 2:3 NIV*

PRAYER LIST	TO DO LIST
1. _____	1. _____
2. _____	2. _____
3. _____	3. _____
4. _____	4. _____
5. _____	5. _____
6. _____	6. _____
7. _____	7. _____

Prayer journal notes:

Numbers 23-25; Mark 7:14-37

_____

_____

_____

_____

_____

_____

_____

_____

DAY 62

Each day is like an identical suitcase. Make the most out of what you pack in yours.

> *"Be very careful then, how you live-not as unwise but as wise, making the most out of every opportunity."*
>
> Ephesians 5:15-16 NIV

PRAYER LIST	TO DO LIST
1. _____	1. _____
2. _____	2. _____
3. _____	3. _____
4. _____	4. _____
5. _____	5. _____
6. _____	6. _____
7. _____	7. _____

Prayer journal notes:

Numbers 26-28; Mark 8

_____
_____
_____
_____
_____
_____
_____
_____
_____
_____

DAY 63

~⌒~

There is never a wrong time to do what is right.

*"Let us not become weary in doing good, for at the proper
time we will reap a harvest if we do not give up."*

Ephesians 6:9 NIV

PRAYER LIST	TO DO LIST
1. _____	1. _____
2. _____	2. _____
3. _____	3. _____
4. _____	4. _____
5. _____	5. _____
6. _____	6. _____
7. _____	7. _____

Prayer journal notes:

Numbers 29-31; Mark 9:1-29

_____

_____

_____

_____

_____

_____

_____

_____

_____

_____

_____

DAY 64

Be thankful regardless of the situation. Beggars can't be choosers. Someone drowning should not complain about the size of the life preserver.

"Do all things without complaining and disputing."
Philippians 2:14 NKJV

PRAYER LIST	TO DO LIST
1. _____	1. _____
2. _____	2. _____
3. _____	3. _____
4. _____	4. _____
5. _____	5. _____
6. _____	6. _____
7. _____	7. _____

Prayer journal notes:

Numbers 32-34; Mark 9:30-50

_____

_____

_____

_____

_____

_____

_____

_____

_____

_____

DAY 65

⌒◯

God gives His children the desire, and then blesses them by fulfilling it.

"May He give you the desire of your heart and make all your plans succeed."

Psalm 20:4 NIV

PRAYER LIST	TO DO LIST
1. _____	1. _____
2. _____	2. _____
3. _____	3. _____
4. _____	4. _____
5. _____	5. _____
6. _____	6. _____
7. _____	7. _____

Prayer journal notes:

Numbers 35-36; Mark 10:1-31

_____
_____
_____
_____
_____
_____
_____
_____
_____

DAY 66

When God waits, it's for a reason. He is never in a hurry, and always on time.

> *"So that God's Son may be glorified...when He heard that Lazarus was sick, He stayed where He was for two more days."*
>
> *John 11:4-6 NIV*

PRAYER LIST	TO DO LIST
1. _____	1. _____
2. _____	2. _____
3. _____	3. _____
4. _____	4. _____
5. _____	5. _____
6. _____	6. _____
7. _____	7. _____

Prayer journal notes:

Deuteronomy 1-3; Mark 10:32-52

_____

_____

_____

_____

_____

_____

_____

_____

DAY 67

God holds to a higher accountability those who make decisions that affect the entire family. Make them wisely.

"Choose for yourselves this day whom you will serve…
but as for me and my household, we will serve the Lord."
Joshua 24:15 NIV

PRAYER LIST	TO DO LIST
1. _____	1. _____
2. _____	2. _____
3. _____	3. _____
4. _____	4. _____
5. _____	5. _____
6. _____	6. _____
7. _____	7. _____

Prayer journal notes:

Deuteronomy 4-6; Mark 11:1-18

_____

_____

_____

_____

_____

_____

_____

_____

_____

DAY 68

Regardless of the circumstances, there is always hope. Search the scriptures. Claim God's promises for you.

"For everything that was written in the past was written to teach us so that through endurance and the encouragement of the Scriptures, we might have hope."

Romans 15:4 NIV

PRAYER LIST	TO DO LIST
1. _____	1. _____
2. _____	2. _____
3. _____	3. _____
4. _____	4. _____
5. _____	5. _____
6. _____	6. _____
7. _____	7. _____

Prayer journal notes:

Deuteronomy 7-9; Mark 11:19-33

_____

_____

_____

_____

_____

_____

_____

_____

DAY 69

Those who rely on God's strength cannot be broken. His strength is perfect when our strength is gone. He'll carry us when we can't carry on.

"It is God who arms me with strength and makes my way perfect."

2 Samuel 22:33 NIV

PRAYER LIST	TO DO LIST
1. _____	1. _____
2. _____	2. _____
3. _____	3. _____
4. _____	4. _____
5. _____	5. _____
6. _____	6. _____
7. _____	7. _____

Prayer journal notes:

Deuteronomy 10-12; Mark 12:1-27

_____

_____

_____

_____

_____

_____

_____

_____

DAY 70

Whatever your fight today...rest assured you are not fighting alone.

"Do not be afraid of them; the Lord your God Himself will fight for you."

Deuteronomy 3:22 NIV

PRAYER LIST	TO DO LIST
1. _____	1. _____
2. _____	2. _____
3. _____	3. _____
4. _____	4. _____
5. _____	5. _____
6. _____	6. _____
7. _____	7. _____

Prayer journal notes:

Deuteronomy 13-15; Mark 12:28-44

_____

_____

_____

_____

_____

_____

_____

_____

_____

_____

DAY 71

Sometimes things happen in our lives that disrupt our normality, and just aren't good. But somehow, they will work together for good.

"And we know that all things work together for good to those who love God, to those who are the called according to His purpose."

Romans 8:28 NKJV

PRAYER LIST	TO DO LIST
1. _____	1. _____
2. _____	2. _____
3. _____	3. _____
4. _____	4. _____
5. _____	5. _____
6. _____	6. _____
7. _____	7. _____

Prayer journal notes:

Deuteronomy 16-18; Mark 13:1-20

_____

_____

_____

_____

_____

_____

_____

_____

DAY 72

Sometimes clouds prevent us from seeing the beautiful sunrise and sunset that God provides for us each day. The clouds are temporary. God is always there.

> *"I am the Lord; there is no other...I will strengthen you...so that from the rising of the sun to the place of its setting...all may know there is none besides Me."*
>
> *Isaiah 45:5-6 NIV*

PRAYER LIST	TO DO LIST
1. _____	1. _____
2. _____	2. _____
3. _____	3. _____
4. _____	4. _____
5. _____	5. _____
6. _____	6. _____
7. _____	7. _____

Prayer journal notes:

Deuteronomy 19-21; Mark 13:21-37

_____

_____

_____

_____

_____

_____

_____

_____

DAY 73

◈

Don't allow things that are good to consume so much of your time that they keep you from things that are better.

"Martha was distracted by all the preparations that had to be made...Mary sat at the Lord's feet listening to what He said...Mary has chosen what is better."
Luke 10:38-42 NIV

PRAYER LIST	TO DO LIST
1. _____	1. _____
2. _____	2. _____
3. _____	3. _____
4. _____	4. _____
5. _____	5. _____
6. _____	6. _____
7. _____	7. _____

Prayer journal notes:

Deuteronomy 22-24; Mark 14:1-26

_____

_____

_____

_____

_____

_____

_____

DAY 74

Always think and speak carefully. Your words and thoughts have an amazing potential to make God smile.

> *"May the words of my mouth and the meditation of my heart be pleasing in your sight, O Lord, my Rock and my Redeemer."*
>
> Psalm 19:14 NIV

PRAYER LIST	TO DO LIST
1. _____	1. _____
2. _____	2. _____
3. _____	3. _____
4. _____	4. _____
5. _____	5. _____
6. _____	6. _____
7. _____	7. _____

Prayer journal notes:

Deuteronomy 25-27; Mark 14:27-53

_____

_____

_____

_____

_____

_____

_____

_____

DAY 75

Not sure who is the most delighted, God or us, when we take refuge in Him.

> *"Let all who take refuge in You be glad; let them ever sing for joy. Spread your protection over them, that those who love Your name may rejoice in You."*
>
> *Psalm 5:11 NIV*

PRAYER LIST	TO DO LIST
1. _____	1. _____
2. _____	2. _____
3. _____	3. _____
4. _____	4. _____
5. _____	5. _____
6. _____	6. _____
7. _____	7. _____

Prayer journal notes:

Deuteronomy 28-29; Mark 14:54-72

_____
_____
_____
_____
_____
_____
_____
_____

DAY 76

You never outgrow, graduate or retire from serving. God demands more from you when He sees more in you.

"From everyone who has been given much, much will be demanded; and from the one who has been entrusted with much, much more will be asked."

Luke 12:48 NIV

PRAYER LIST	TO DO LIST
1. _____	1. _____
2. _____	2. _____
3. _____	3. _____
4. _____	4. _____
5. _____	5. _____
6. _____	6. _____
7. _____	7. _____

Prayer journal notes:

Deuteronomy 30-31; Mark 15:1-25

_____

_____

_____

_____

_____

_____

_____

_____

DAY 77

〜◯〜

The Bible is the best-selling book of all time, but the least read. It is there we can find God's answers for any problems we may face. It is our guide for living.

> *"Take heart to all these words...they are not just idle words for you...they are your life."*
> *Deuteronomy 32:46-47 NIV*

PRAYER LIST	TO DO LIST
1. _____	1. _____
2. _____	2. _____
3. _____	3. _____
4. _____	4. _____
5. _____	5. _____
6. _____	6. _____
7. _____	7. _____

Prayer journal notes:

Deuteronomy 32-34; Mark 15:26-47

_____
_____
_____
_____
_____
_____
_____
_____

DAY 78

You can cancel church services, but not the church. The church is not the building but the body, the people. Now, more than ever, we must BE the church.

"And Christ is the head of the body, the church..."
Colossians 1:18 NIV

PRAYER LIST	TO DO LIST
1. _____	1. _____
2. _____	2. _____
3. _____	3. _____
4. _____	4. _____
5. _____	5. _____
6. _____	6. _____
7. _____	7. _____

Prayer journal notes:

Joshua 1-3; Mark 16

_____

_____

_____

_____

_____

_____

_____

_____

_____

DAY 79

❧

Regardless of a quarantine or isolation, we never have to walk alone.

"Since we live by the Spirit, let us keep in step with the Spirit."

Galatians 5:25 NIV

PRAYER LIST	TO DO LIST
1. _____	1. _____
2. _____	2. _____
3. _____	3. _____
4. _____	4. _____
5. _____	5. _____
6. _____	6. _____
7. _____	7. _____

Prayer journal notes:

Joshua 4-6; Luke 1:1-20

_____

_____

_____

_____

_____

_____

_____

_____

DAY 80

When we fear the Lord, we have no need to fear anyone or anything else.

> *"The Lord is my light and my salvation-whom shall I fear? The Lord is the stronghold of my life-of whom shall I be afraid?"*
>
> Psalm 27:1 NIV

PRAYER LIST	TO DO LIST
1. _____	1. _____
2. _____	2. _____
3. _____	3. _____
4. _____	4. _____
5. _____	5. _____
6. _____	6. _____
7. _____	7. _____

Prayer journal notes:

Joshua 7-9; Luke 1:21-38

_____

_____

_____

_____

_____

_____

_____

_____

DAY 81

The God of Abraham, Isaac, and Jacob is our God. The God of Peter, James, and John is our God. Our God is an awesome God! He reigns from heaven above. With wisdom, power and love, our God is an awesome God!

"The Lord Almighty is with us; the God of Jacob is our fortress."

Psalm 46:11 NIV

PRAYER LIST	TO DO LIST
1. _____	1. _____
2. _____	2. _____
3. _____	3. _____
4. _____	4. _____
5. _____	5. _____
6. _____	6. _____
7. _____	7. _____

Prayer journal notes:

Joshua 10-12; Luke 1:39-56

_____

_____

_____

_____

_____

_____

_____

_____

DAY 82

Faith involves knowing that God is enough; that when He's all we've got, He's all we need.

"The Lord who delivered me from the paw of the lion and the paw of the bear will deliver me from the hand of this Philistine."

1 Samuel 17:37 NIV

PRAYER LIST	TO DO LIST
1. _____	1. _____
2. _____	2. _____
3. _____	3. _____
4. _____	4. _____
5. _____	5. _____
6. _____	6. _____
7. _____	7. _____

Prayer journal notes:

Joshua 13-15; Luke 1:57-80

_____

_____

_____

_____

_____

_____

_____

_____

DAY 83

When we choose to make money our god, our value of life decreases just like the value of the dollar.

"For the love of money is a root of all kinds of evil."
1 Timothy 6:10 NIV

PRAYER LIST	TO DO LIST
1. _____	1. _____
2. _____	2. _____
3. _____	3. _____
4. _____	4. _____
5. _____	5. _____
6. _____	6. _____
7. _____	7. _____

Prayer journal notes:

Joshua 16-18; Luke 2:1-24

_____
_____
_____
_____
_____
_____
_____
_____
_____
_____

DAY 84

God's Word is full of His promises-and He is committed to keeping every one.

"The Lord is faithful to all His promises..."

Psalm 145:13 NIV

PRAYER LIST	TO DO LIST
1. _____	1. _____
2. _____	2. _____
3. _____	3. _____
4. _____	4. _____
5. _____	5. _____
6. _____	6. _____
7. _____	7. _____

Prayer journal notes:

Joshua 19-21; Luke 2:25-52

_____
_____
_____
_____
_____
_____
_____
_____
_____
_____
_____

DAY 85

You have weapons at your disposal that your enemies, including Satan, are no match for.

> *"The weapons we fight with are not the weapons of the world. On the contrary, they have divine power to demolish strongholds."*
>
> *2 Corinthians 10:4 NIV*

PRAYER LIST	TO DO LIST
1. _____	1. _____
2. _____	2. _____
3. _____	3. _____
4. _____	4. _____
5. _____	5. _____
6. _____	6. _____
7. _____	7. _____

Prayer journal notes:

Joshua 22-24; Luke 3

_____

_____

_____

_____

_____

_____

_____

_____

DAY 86

God not only helps us. He helps us help others. We help others by helping them help themselves.

> *"Do not be dismayed, for I am your God. I will strengthen you and help you."*
>
> Isaiah 41:10 NIV

PRAYER LIST	TO DO LIST
1. _____	1. _____
2. _____	2. _____
3. _____	3. _____
4. _____	4. _____
5. _____	5. _____
6. _____	6. _____
7. _____	7. _____

Prayer journal notes:

Judges 1-3; Luke 4:1-30

_____

_____

_____

_____

_____

_____

_____

_____

_____

DAY 87

Sometimes it is very difficult to communicate effectively. There is much less strain on communicating face-to-face if you are walking side-by-side.

"If we walk in the light as He is in the light, we have fellowship with one another..."

1 John 1:7 NIV

PRAYER LIST	TO DO LIST
1. _____	1. _____
2. _____	2. _____
3. _____	3. _____
4. _____	4. _____
5. _____	5. _____
6. _____	6. _____
7. _____	7. _____

Prayer journal notes:

Judges 4-6; Luke 4:31-44

_____
_____
_____
_____
_____
_____
_____
_____

DAY 88

Jesus was severely mistreated and had every reason to be angry and resentful when He was beaten and hung on the cross. If we could just act as He did when we are mistreated.

"Jesus said, 'Father, forgive them, for they do not know what they are doing.'"

Luke 23:34 NIV

PRAYER LIST	TO DO LIST
1. _____	1. _____
2. _____	2. _____
3. _____	3. _____
4. _____	4. _____
5. _____	5. _____
6. _____	6. _____
7. _____	7. _____

Prayer journal notes:

Judges 7-8; Luke 5:1-16

_____

_____

_____

_____

_____

_____

_____

_____

DAY 89

There is always light at the end of the tunnel when heaven is your final destination.

"The people walking in darkness have seen a great light…a light has dawned."

Isaiah 9:2 NIV

PRAYER LIST	TO DO LIST
1. _____	1. _____
2. _____	2. _____
3. _____	3. _____
4. _____	4. _____
5. _____	5. _____
6. _____	6. _____
7. _____	7. _____

Prayer journal notes:

Judges 9-10; Luke 5:17-39

_____

_____

_____

_____

_____

_____

_____

_____

DAY 90

Jesus didn't have to die but He chose to so we won't have to.

"Jesus said to her, 'I am the resurrection and the life. He who believes in Me will live, even though he dies, and whoever lives and believes in Me will never die.'"

John 11:25-26 NIV

PRAYER LIST	TO DO LIST
1. _____	1. _____
2. _____	2. _____
3. _____	3. _____
4. _____	4. _____
5. _____	5. _____
6. _____	6. _____
7. _____	7. _____

Prayer journal notes:

Judges 11-12; Luke 6:1-26

_____

_____

_____

_____

_____

_____

_____

_____

_____

DAY 91

⌒◦⌒

The difference between our God and other gods is that the grave couldn't hold ours.

"He is not here; He has risen, just as He said."
Matthew 28:6 NIV

PRAYER LIST	TO DO LIST
1. _____	1. _____
2. _____	2. _____
3. _____	3. _____
4. _____	4. _____
5. _____	5. _____
6. _____	6. _____
7. _____	7. _____

Prayer journal notes:

Judges 13-15; Luke 6:27-49

_____

_____

_____

_____

_____

_____

_____

_____

_____

_____

_____

DAY 92

Failure is an event, never a person. A failing event in your life is beneficial when it causes you to lean on and love Jesus more.

> *"The Lord is close to the brokenhearted and saves those who are crushed in spirit."*
>
> *Psalm 34:18 NIV*

PRAYER LIST	TO DO LIST
1. _____	1. _____
2. _____	2. _____
3. _____	3. _____
4. _____	4. _____
5. _____	5. _____
6. _____	6. _____
7. _____	7. _____

Prayer journal notes:

Judges 16-18; Luke 7:1-30

_____

_____

_____

_____

_____

_____

_____

_____

_____

DAY 93

Sometimes the outlook may seem grim, but keep the faith. We don't live by explanations, but by promises. Jesus keeps His.

"After three days, I will rise again."

Matthew 27:63 NIV

PRAYER LIST	TO DO LIST
1. _____	1. _____
2. _____	2. _____
3. _____	3. _____
4. _____	4. _____
5. _____	5. _____
6. _____	6. _____
7. _____	7. _____

Prayer journal notes:

Judges 19-21; Luke 7:31-50

_____

_____

_____

_____

_____

_____

_____

_____

_____

_____

DAY 94

We do not have to prove God's existence to anyone because no one can disprove it.

"Do you not know? Have you not heard? The Lord is the everlasting God, the Creator of the ends of the earth. He will not grow tired or weary, and His understanding no one can fathom."

Isaiah 40:28 NIV

PRAYER LIST	TO DO LIST
1. _____	1. _____
2. _____	2. _____
3. _____	3. _____
4. _____	4. _____
5. _____	5. _____
6. _____	6. _____
7. _____	7. _____

Prayer journal notes:

Ruth 1-4; Luke 8:1-25

_____

_____

_____

_____

_____

_____

_____

_____

DAY 95

Our faith is not based on a dead prophet. We celebrate the resurrection today and every day.

"Why do you look for the living among the dead? He is not here. He is risen."

Luke 24:5-6 NIV

PRAYER LIST	TO DO LIST
1. _____	1. _____
2. _____	2. _____
3. _____	3. _____
4. _____	4. _____
5. _____	5. _____
6. _____	6. _____
7. _____	7. _____

Prayer journal notes:

I Samuel 1-3; Luke 8:26-56

_____

_____

_____

_____

_____

_____

_____

_____

_____

DAY 96

The generous person always has more than enough, but the greedy person never has enough.

"It is more blessed to give than to receive."

Acts 20:35 NIV

PRAYER LIST	TO DO LIST
1. _____	1. _____
2. _____	2. _____
3. _____	3. _____
4. _____	4. _____
5. _____	5. _____
6. _____	6. _____
7. _____	7. _____

Prayer journal notes:

I Samuel 4-6; Luke 9:1-17

_____

_____

_____

_____

_____

_____

_____

_____

_____

_____

_____

DAY 97

Prayer is always important, never outdated, and something
we can never outgrow or short cut with technology.

*"For the eyes of the Lord are on the righteous and His
ears are attentive to their prayer."*

1 Peter 3:12 NIV

PRAYER LIST	TO DO LIST
1. _____	1. _____
2. _____	2. _____
3. _____	3. _____
4. _____	4. _____
5. _____	5. _____
6. _____	6. _____
7. _____	7. _____

Prayer journal notes:

1 Samuel 7-9; Luke 9:18-36

_____

_____

_____

_____

_____

_____

_____

_____

DAY 98

Setting a good example is much better than giving good advice. "Do as I say and not as I do," has no validity.

> *"If God has given you leadership ability, take the responsibility seriously."*
>
> Romans 12:8 NLT

PRAYER LIST	TO DO LIST
1. _____	1. _____
2. _____	2. _____
3. _____	3. _____
4. _____	4. _____
5. _____	5. _____
6. _____	6. _____
7. _____	7. _____

Prayer journal notes:

I Samuel 10-12; Luke 9:37-62

_____

_____

_____

_____

_____

_____

_____

_____

_____

DAY 99

∽⊙

God solving your problems is a good thing if you grow closer to Him as a result.

"Praise be to God…who comforts us in all our troubles…"
2 Corinthians 1:3 NIV

PRAYER LIST	TO DO LIST
1. _____	1. _____
2. _____	2. _____
3. _____	3. _____
4. _____	4. _____
5. _____	5. _____
6. _____	6. _____
7. _____	7. _____

Prayer journal notes:

I Samuel 13-14; Luke 10:1-24

_____
_____
_____
_____
_____
_____
_____
_____
_____
_____

DAY 100

Children laugh much more than adults. Laughter is biblical. Don't allow growing old to keep you from laughing.

"We are filled with laughter and we sang for joy."

Psalm 126:2 NLT

PRAYER LIST	TO DO LIST
1. _____	1. _____
2. _____	2. _____
3. _____	3. _____
4. _____	4. _____
5. _____	5. _____
6. _____	6. _____
7. _____	7. _____

Prayer journal notes:

I Samuel 15-16; Luke 10:25-42

_____

_____

_____

_____

_____

_____

_____

_____

_____

_____

DAY 101

You are much more thankful for what you have when you can clearly remember having a whole lot less.

"Be joyful always; pray continually; give thanks in all circumstances, for this is God's will for you in Christ Jesus."

1 Thessalonians 5:16-18 NIV

PRAYER LIST	TO DO LIST
1. _____	1. _____
2. _____	2. _____
3. _____	3. _____
4. _____	4. _____
5. _____	5. _____
6. _____	6. _____
7. _____	7. _____

Prayer journal notes:

I Samuel 17-18; Luke 11:1-28

_____

_____

_____

_____

_____

_____

_____

_____

DAY 102

In times of crises, one of the best things we can do to be strengthened is to turn to the One with limitless strength.

> *"That you may live a life worthy of the Lord...being strengthened with all power..."*
>
> Colossians 1:10-11 NIV

PRAYER LIST	TO DO LIST
1. _____	1. _____
2. _____	2. _____
3. _____	3. _____
4. _____	4. _____
5. _____	5. _____
6. _____	6. _____
7. _____	7. _____

Prayer journal notes:

I Samuel 19-21; Luke 11:29-54

_____

_____

_____

_____

_____

_____

_____

_____

_____

DAY 103

We are only stewards, managers of our money. Manage your money as if every cent belongs to God, because it does.

"You cannot serve both God and money."

Luke 16:13 NIV

PRAYER LIST	TO DO LIST
1. _____	1. _____
2. _____	2. _____
3. _____	3. _____
4. _____	4. _____
5. _____	5. _____
6. _____	6. _____
7. _____	7. _____

Prayer journal notes:

I Samuel 22-24; Luke 12:1-31

_____

_____

_____

_____

_____

_____

_____

_____

_____

_____

DAY 104

Spending time with a child is priceless. You will never see a tombstone that says, "I wish I hadn't spent so much time with my children."

> *"Children are a gift from the Lord. They are a reward from Him."*
>
> Psalm 127:3 NLT

PRAYER LIST	TO DO LIST
1. _____	1. _____
2. _____	2. _____
3. _____	3. _____
4. _____	4. _____
5. _____	5. _____
6. _____	6. _____
7. _____	7. _____

Prayer journal notes:

I Samuel 25-26; Luke 12:32-59

_____

_____

_____

_____

_____

_____

_____

_____

DAY 105

Your care for others is a measure of your greatness. The only time to ever look down at someone is to help them up.

"If you think you are too important to help someone in need, you are only fooling yourself."

Galatians 6:3 NLT

PRAYER LIST	TO DO LIST
1. _____	1. _____
2. _____	2. _____
3. _____	3. _____
4. _____	4. _____
5. _____	5. _____
6. _____	6. _____
7. _____	7. _____

Prayer journal notes:

I Samuel 27-29; Luke 13:1-22

_____

_____

_____

_____

_____

_____

_____

_____

_____

DAY 106

Don't ask God to lead you where He wants you to go if you are not willing to go where He wants to lead you.

> *"Hear my cry O God...lead me to the Rock that is higher."*
>
> Psalm 61:1-2 NIV

PRAYER LIST	TO DO LIST
1. _____	1. _____
2. _____	2. _____
3. _____	3. _____
4. _____	4. _____
5. _____	5. _____
6. _____	6. _____
7. _____	7. _____

Prayer journal notes:

I Samuel 30-31; Luke 13:23-35

_____
_____
_____
_____
_____
_____
_____
_____
_____

DAY 107

The best place to go for comfort from heartache is to the ultimate Comforter.

"For the Lord comforts His people…"

Isaiah 49:13 NIV

PRAYER LIST	TO DO LIST
1. _____	1. _____
2. _____	2. _____
3. _____	3. _____
4. _____	4. _____
5. _____	5. _____
6. _____	6. _____
7. _____	7. _____

Prayer journal notes:

II Samuel 1-2; Luke 14:1-24

_____

_____

_____

_____

_____

_____

_____

_____

_____

_____

DAY 108

When evil raises its ugly head and seems to have won the battle, never forget who is going to ultimately win the war.

"I am the Alpha and the Omega...who is and who was and who is to come, the Almighty"

Revelation 1:8 NIV

PRAYER LIST	TO DO LIST
1. _____	1. _____
2. _____	2. _____
3. _____	3. _____
4. _____	4. _____
5. _____	5. _____
6. _____	6. _____
7. _____	7. _____

Prayer journal notes:

II Samuel 3-5; Luke 14:25-35

_____

_____

_____

_____

_____

_____

_____

_____

_____

DAY 109

When the waves get rough and the storm gets tough, those dependent upon Christ have the amazing ability to hold their ship steady and ride the storm out.

> *"We have this hope as an anchor for the soul, firm and secure."*
>
> *Hebrews 6:19 NIV*

PRAYER LIST	TO DO LIST
1. _____	1. _____
2. _____	2. _____
3. _____	3. _____
4. _____	4. _____
5. _____	5. _____
6. _____	6. _____
7. _____	7. _____

Prayer journal notes:

II Samuel 6-8; Luke 15:1-10

_____
_____
_____
_____
_____
_____
_____
_____

DAY 110

We don't need more to be thankful for, we just need to be more thankful. Count your blessings, see what God has done!

"Let them give thanks to the Lord for His unfailing love and His wonderful deeds."

Psalm 107:21 NIV

PRAYER LIST	TO DO LIST
1. _____	1. _____
2. _____	2. _____
3. _____	3. _____
4. _____	4. _____
5. _____	5. _____
6. _____	6. _____
7. _____	7. _____

Prayer journal notes:

II Samuel 9-11; Luke 15:11-32

_____

_____

_____

_____

_____

_____

_____

_____

_____

DAY 111

No matter who you are or what you do, you will always be essential in God's eyes.

"And the very hairs of your head are all numbered."
Matthew 10:30 NIV

PRAYER LIST	TO DO LIST
1. _____	1. _____
2. _____	2. _____
3. _____	3. _____
4. _____	4. _____
5. _____	5. _____
6. _____	6. _____
7. _____	7. _____

Prayer journal notes:

II Samuel 12-13; Luke 16

_____

_____

_____

_____

_____

_____

_____

_____

_____

_____

DAY 112

A good friend can multiply your joy and divide your sorrow. It's never too late to renew an old friendship. Give an old friend a call today!

"An old friend is always loyal."

Proverbs 17:17 NLT

PRAYER LIST	TO DO LIST
1. _____	1. _____
2. _____	2. _____
3. _____	3. _____
4. _____	4. _____
5. _____	5. _____
6. _____	6. _____
7. _____	7. _____

Prayer journal notes:

II Samuel 14-15; Luke 17:1-19

_____

_____

_____

_____

_____

_____

_____

_____

_____

DAY 113

God talks to His children. If you don't hear Him, there may be a reason.

> *"He who belongs to God hears what God says. The reason you do not hear is that you do not belong to God."*
> *John 8:47 NIV*

PRAYER LIST	TO DO LIST
1. _____	1. _____
2. _____	2. _____
3. _____	3. _____
4. _____	4. _____
5. _____	5. _____
6. _____	6. _____
7. _____	7. _____

Prayer journal notes:

II Samuel 16-18; Luke 17:20-37

_____
_____
_____
_____
_____
_____
_____
_____
_____

DAY 114

Be stingy with criticism and generous with praise. To belittle
is to be little.

*"Do not judge or you too will be judged. For in the same
way you judge others, you will be judged."*

Matthew 7:1-2 NIV

PRAYER LIST	TO DO LIST
1. _____	1. _____
2. _____	2. _____
3. _____	3. _____
4. _____	4. _____
5. _____	5. _____
6. _____	6. _____
7. _____	7. _____

Prayer journal notes:

II Samuel 19-20; Luke 18:1-23

_____

_____

_____

_____

_____

_____

_____

_____

_____

_____

DAY 115

Spend more time with people who bless you and less time with people who stress you.

> "What does righteousness and wickedness have in common? Or what fellowship can light have with darkness?"
>
> *2 Corinthians 6:14 NIV*

PRAYER LIST	TO DO LIST
1. _____	1. _____
2. _____	2. _____
3. _____	3. _____
4. _____	4. _____
5. _____	5. _____
6. _____	6. _____
7. _____	7. _____

Prayer journal notes:

II Samuel 21-22; Luke 18:24-43

_____
_____
_____
_____
_____
_____
_____
_____

DAY 116

A decision based on emotion is a short-term action that can have long-term consequences.

"A fool gives full vent to his anger, but a wise man keeps himself under control."

Proverbs 29:11 NIV

PRAYER LIST	TO DO LIST
1. _____	1. _____
2. _____	2. _____
3. _____	3. _____
4. _____	4. _____
5. _____	5. _____
6. _____	6. _____
7. _____	7. _____

Prayer journal notes:

II Samuel 23-24; Luke 19:1-27

_____

_____

_____

_____

_____

_____

_____

_____

_____

DAY 117

Whatever you are up against today; maybe that EGR (extra grace required) family member or colleague at work — your God is greater!

> *"The One who is in you is greater than the One who is in the world."*
>
> *1 John 4:4 NIV*

PRAYER LIST	TO DO LIST
1. _____	1. _____
2. _____	2. _____
3. _____	3. _____
4. _____	4. _____
5. _____	5. _____
6. _____	6. _____
7. _____	7. _____

Prayer journal notes:

I Kings 1-2; Luke 19:28-48

_____
_____
_____
_____
_____
_____
_____
_____

DAY 118

Don't allow anyone to bring you down. You lift them up!

> *"Do not be overcome by evil, but overcome evil with good."*
>
> Romans 12:21 NIV

PRAYER LIST

1. _____
2. _____
3. _____
4. _____
5. _____
6. _____
7. _____

TO DO LIST

1. _____
2. _____
3. _____
4. _____
5. _____
6. _____
7. _____

Prayer journal notes:

I Kings 3-5; Luke 20:1-26

_____
_____
_____
_____
_____
_____
_____
_____
_____
_____
_____

DAY 119

The best way to show you love Jesus is to love others, especially those who are hard to love.

"By this all men will know that you are my disciples, if you love one another."

John 13:35 NIV

PRAYER LIST	TO DO LIST
1. _____	1. _____
2. _____	2. _____
3. _____	3. _____
4. _____	4. _____
5. _____	5. _____
6. _____	6. _____
7. _____	7. _____

Prayer journal notes:

I Kings 6-7; Luke 20:27-47

_____

_____

_____

_____

_____

_____

_____

_____

_____

DAY 120

Everything happens for a reason. You may not understand God's purpose until later, so don't be disappointed when your will is not done. God knows best. Trust Him.

> *"Trust in the Lord with all your heart and lean not on your own understanding; in all your ways acknowledge Him, and He will make your paths straight."*
>
> *Proverbs 3:5-6 NIV*

PRAYER LIST	TO DO LIST
1. _____	1. _____
2. _____	2. _____
3. _____	3. _____
4. _____	4. _____
5. _____	5. _____
6. _____	6. _____
7. _____	7. _____

Prayer journal notes:

I Kings 8-9; Luke 21:1-19

_____
_____
_____
_____
_____
_____
_____
_____

DAY 121

You cannot reach forward and grasp the new things God has for you if your hands are tied up by holding on to what is behind you.

"Forgetting those things which are behind and reaching forward to those things which are ahead, I press on toward the goal for the prize of the upward call of God in Christ Jesus."

Philippians 3:13-14 NKJV

PRAYER LIST	TO DO LIST
1. _____	1. _____
2. _____	2. _____
3. _____	3. _____
4. _____	4. _____
5. _____	5. _____
6. _____	6. _____
7. _____	7. _____

Prayer journal notes:

I Kings 10-11; Luke 21:20-38

_____

_____

_____

_____

_____

_____

_____

DAY 122

God loves you and will lead you in the right direction if you will allow Him to. He will never send someone who is thirsty to a well that is dry.

"Whoever drinks the water I give him will never thirst."

John 4:14 NIV

PRAYER LIST	TO DO LIST
1. _____	1. _____
2. _____	2. _____
3. _____	3. _____
4. _____	4. _____
5. _____	5. _____
6. _____	6. _____
7. _____	7. _____

Prayer journal notes:

I Kings 12-13; Luke 22:1-30

_____

_____

_____

_____

_____

_____

_____

_____

_____

DAY 123

A smile adds to your net worth. It increases your face value. What's in your heart should show on your face.

"A happy heart makes the face cheerful."
Proverbs 15:13 NIV

PRAYER LIST	TO DO LIST
1. _____	1. _____
2. _____	2. _____
3. _____	3. _____
4. _____	4. _____
5. _____	5. _____
6. _____	6. _____
7. _____	7. _____

Prayer journal notes:

I Kings 14-15; Luke 22:31-46

_____
_____
_____
_____
_____
_____
_____
_____
_____
_____
_____

DAY 124

You will never please everyone, so remember to whom you are ultimately accountable.

"Nothing in all creation is hidden from God's sight. Everything is uncovered and laid bare before the eyes of Him to whom we must give account."

Hebrews 4:13 NIV

PRAYER LIST	TO DO LIST
1. _____	1. _____
2. _____	2. _____
3. _____	3. _____
4. _____	4. _____
5. _____	5. _____
6. _____	6. _____
7. _____	7. _____

Prayer journal notes:

I Kings 16-18; Luke 22:47-71

_____
_____
_____
_____
_____
_____
_____
_____

DAY 125

Jesus was never elected to a political office, never led a company, never wrote a book on leadership, but set the example, as the greatest leader in history; you must be willing to serve.

"But I am among you as One who serves."

Luke 22:27 NIV

PRAYER LIST	TO DO LIST
1. _____	1. _____
2. _____	2. _____
3. _____	3. _____
4. _____	4. _____
5. _____	5. _____
6. _____	6. _____
7. _____	7. _____

Prayer journal notes:

I Kings 19-20; Luke 23:1-25

_____

_____

_____

_____

_____

_____

_____

DAY 126

When comforting others, they may not remember what you said, but will remember what you did.

"We continuously remember...your labor prompted by love."

1 Thessalonians 1:3 NIV

PRAYER LIST	TO DO LIST
1. _____	1. _____
2. _____	2. _____
3. _____	3. _____
4. _____	4. _____
5. _____	5. _____
6. _____	6. _____
7. _____	7. _____

Prayer journal notes:

I Kings 21-22; Luke 23:26-56

_____

_____

_____

_____

_____

_____

_____

_____

_____

DAY 127

The greatest joy a parent can have is to know that their child is walking closely with God.

"I have no greater joy than to hear that my children are walking in the truth."

3 John 4 NIV

PRAYER LIST	TO DO LIST
1. _____	1. _____
2. _____	2. _____
3. _____	3. _____
4. _____	4. _____
5. _____	5. _____
6. _____	6. _____
7. _____	7. _____

Prayer journal notes:

II Kings 1-3; Luke 24:1-35

_____

_____

_____

_____

_____

_____

_____

_____

_____

DAY 128

You show others what you believe by the way you behave.

"Just as He who called you is holy, so be holy in all you do."

1 Peter 1:15

PRAYER LIST	TO DO LIST
1. _____	1. _____
2. _____	2. _____
3. _____	3. _____
4. _____	4. _____
5. _____	5. _____
6. _____	6. _____
7. _____	7. _____

Prayer journal notes:

II Kings 4-6; Luke 24:36-53

_____
_____
_____
_____
_____
_____
_____
_____
_____
_____
_____

DAY 129

When someone tells you that you can't do something, they must not know your God.

"I can do all things through Christ who strengthens me."
Philippians 4:13 NKJV

PRAYER LIST	TO DO LIST
1. _____	1. _____
2. _____	2. _____
3. _____	3. _____
4. _____	4. _____
5. _____	5. _____
6. _____	6. _____
7. _____	7. _____

Prayer journal notes:

II Kings 7-9; John 1:1-28

_____
_____
_____
_____
_____
_____
_____
_____
_____
_____
_____

DAY 130

Encouragement is one of the best gifts you can give. Its free, requires no shopping, needs no gift wrapping, can be custom designed, doesn't require batteries, and lasts a lifetime.

> *"Encourage one another daily, as long as it is called 'Today.'..."*
>
> *Hebrews 3:13 NIV*

PRAYER LIST	TO DO LIST
1. _____	1. _____
2. _____	2. _____
3. _____	3. _____
4. _____	4. _____
5. _____	5. _____
6. _____	6. _____
7. _____	7. _____

Prayer journal notes:

II Kings 10-12; John 1:29-51

_____
_____
_____
_____
_____
_____
_____
_____

DAY 131

Although God wants you to walk closely with Him today, He won't force you to. You have to want to.

"You will seek Me and find Me when you seek Me with all your heart."

Jeremiah 29:13 NIV

PRAYER LIST	TO DO LIST
1. _____	1. _____
2. _____	2. _____
3. _____	3. _____
4. _____	4. _____
5. _____	5. _____
6. _____	6. _____
7. _____	7. _____

Prayer journal notes:

II Kings 13-14; John 2

_____
_____
_____
_____
_____
_____
_____
_____
_____

DAY 132

Mothers are an extension of God's love. Next to God's love, a mother's love is the purest form of love one will ever know.

"There she who was in labor gave you birth."
Song of Songs 8:5 NIV

PRAYER LIST	TO DO LIST
1. _____	1. _____
2. _____	2. _____
3. _____	3. _____
4. _____	4. _____
5. _____	5. _____
6. _____	6. _____
7. _____	7. _____

Prayer journal notes:

II Kings 15-16; John 3:1-18

_____
_____
_____
_____
_____
_____
_____
_____
_____
_____

DAY 133

No one is poor who had a Godly mother.
(Abraham Lincoln)

Honor your father and your mother..."

Exodus 20:12 NIV

PRAYER LIST	TO DO LIST
1. _____	1. _____
2. _____	2. _____
3. _____	3. _____
4. _____	4. _____
5. _____	5. _____
6. _____	6. _____
7. _____	7. _____

Prayer journal notes:

II Kings 17-18; John 3:19-36

_____
_____
_____
_____
_____
_____
_____
_____
_____
_____
_____

DAY 134

Live today on purpose, not by accident. Don't let anyone stop you from enjoying God's favor and the abundant life He has for you today.

"Blessed are those whose strength is in You..."
Psalm 84:5 NIV

PRAYER LIST	TO DO LIST
1. _____	1. _____
2. _____	2. _____
3. _____	3. _____
4. _____	4. _____
5. _____	5. _____
6. _____	6. _____
7. _____	7. _____

Prayer journal notes:

II Kings 19-21; John 4:1-30

_____

_____

_____

_____

_____

_____

_____

_____

_____

DAY 135

Nothing in our lives is too small for God to be involved. When He is involved in the small things, our daily grind is meaningful and with purpose.

"This is the day the Lord has made; let us rejoice and be glad in it."

Psalm 118:24 NIV

PRAYER LIST	TO DO LIST
1. _____	1. _____
2. _____	2. _____
3. _____	3. _____
4. _____	4. _____
5. _____	5. _____
6. _____	6. _____
7. _____	7. _____

Prayer journal notes:

II Kings 22-23; John 4:31-54

_____
_____
_____
_____
_____
_____
_____
_____

DAY 136

Make choices today that your future self and family will be glad that you did.

"Choose life, so that you and your children may live."
Deuteronomy 30:19 NIV

PRAYER LIST	TO DO LIST
1. _____	1. _____
2. _____	2. _____
3. _____	3. _____
4. _____	4. _____
5. _____	5. _____
6. _____	6. _____
7. _____	7. _____

Prayer journal notes:

II Kings 24-25; John 5:1-24

_____

_____

_____

_____

_____

_____

_____

_____

_____

_____

_____

DAY 137

Your choice of attitude is directly related to the kind of day you will have:

Good attitude = Good day
Bad attitude = Bad day

"Your attitude should be the same as that of Christ Jesus."
Philippians 2:5 NIV

PRAYER LIST	TO DO LIST
1. _____	1. _____
2. _____	2. _____
3. _____	3. _____
4. _____	4. _____
5. _____	5. _____
6. _____	6. _____
7. _____	7. _____

Prayer journal notes:

I Chronicles 1-3; John 5:25-47

_____
_____
_____
_____
_____
_____
_____
_____

DAY 138

Know where the path you are taking is leading you. It does no good to be making good time and to be going the wrong way.

"It is not good to have zeal without knowledge nor to be hasty and miss the way."

Proverbs 19:2 NIV

PRAYER LIST	TO DO LIST
1. _____	1. _____
2. _____	2. _____
3. _____	3. _____
4. _____	4. _____
5. _____	5. _____
6. _____	6. _____
7. _____	7. _____

Prayer journal notes:

I Chronicles 4-6; John 6:1-21

_____

_____

_____

_____

_____

_____

_____

_____

_____

DAY 139

～◌

Don't complain about where you are if you unwilling to move to improve.

"Jesus asked, 'Do you want to get well?"

John 5:6 NIV

PRAYER LIST	TO DO LIST
1. _____	1. _____
2. _____	2. _____
3. _____	3. _____
4. _____	4. _____
5. _____	5. _____
6. _____	6. _____
7. _____	7. _____

Prayer journal notes:

I Chronicles 7-9; John 6:22-44

_____
_____
_____
_____
_____
_____
_____
_____
_____
_____

DAY 140

❦

The first step to improving a weakness is to acknowledge that you have it.

"No dear brothers, I am still not all I should be..."
Philippians 3:13 TLB

PRAYER LIST	TO DO LIST
1. _____	1. _____
2. _____	2. _____
3. _____	3. _____
4. _____	4. _____
5. _____	5. _____
6. _____	6. _____
7. _____	7. _____

Prayer journal notes:

I Chronicles 10-12; John 6:45-71

_____

_____

_____

_____

_____

_____

_____

_____

_____

_____

_____

DAY 141

Something becomes worthwhile when it moves from your head to your heart to your hands.

> *"Lazy hands make a poor man, but diligent hands bring wealth."*
>
> *Proverbs 10:4 NIV*

PRAYER LIST	TO DO LIST
1. _____	1. _____
2. _____	2. _____
3. _____	3. _____
4. _____	4. _____
5. _____	5. _____
6. _____	6. _____
7. _____	7. _____

Prayer journal notes:

I Chronicles 13-15; John 7:1-27

_____

_____

_____

_____

_____

_____

_____

_____

DAY 142

While others may see what we do, God sees our heart and why we do it.

"Your Father who sees in secret will reward you openly."
Matthew 6:18 NKJV

PRAYER LIST	TO DO LIST
1. _____	1. _____
2. _____	2. _____
3. _____	3. _____
4. _____	4. _____
5. _____	5. _____
6. _____	6. _____
7. _____	7. _____

Prayer journal notes:

I Chronicles 16-18; John 7:28-53

_____

_____

_____

_____

_____

_____

_____

_____

_____

_____

DAY 143

Some people will miss heaven by about 18 inches; the distance between their head to their heart. Knowing about Jesus is not the same as knowing Him personally. Satan and all his demons know about Him.

"The man who says, 'I know Him,' but does not do what He commands is a liar and the truth is not in him."

I John 2:3 NIV

PRAYER LIST	TO DO LIST
1. _____	1. _____
2. _____	2. _____
3. _____	3. _____
4. _____	4. _____
5. _____	5. _____
6. _____	6. _____
7. _____	7. _____

Prayer journal notes:

I Chronicles 19-21; John 8:1-27

_____

_____

_____

_____

_____

_____

_____

_____

DAY 144

Take all the pieces of your broken heart to God. He specializes in heart transplants.

> *"I will give you a new heart and put a new spirit in you; I will remove from you a heart of stone and give you a heart of flesh."*
>
> *Ezekiel 36:26 NIV*

PRAYER LIST	TO DO LIST
1. _____	1. _____
2. _____	2. _____
3. _____	3. _____
4. _____	4. _____
5. _____	5. _____
6. _____	6. _____
7. _____	7. _____

Prayer journal notes:

I Chronicles 22-24; John 8:28-59

_____
_____
_____
_____
_____
_____
_____
_____

DAY 145

Our level of peace is determined by where our mind is focused.

> *"You keep him in perfect peace whose mind is stayed on you."*
>
> *Isaiah 26:3 NKJV*

PRAYER LIST	TO DO LIST
1. _____	1. _____
2. _____	2. _____
3. _____	3. _____
4. _____	4. _____
5. _____	5. _____
6. _____	6. _____
7. _____	7. _____

Prayer journal notes:

I Chronicles 25-27; John 9:1-23

_____

_____

_____

_____

_____

_____

_____

_____

DAY 146

Every day something in this world never ceases to amaze us, but not God. He made it all. He's seen it all. He simply says, "Been there, done that."

"Before the mountains were born or you brought forth the earth and the world, from everlasting to everlasting you are God."

Psalm 90:2 NIV

PRAYER LIST	TO DO LIST
1. _____	1. _____
2. _____	2. _____
3. _____	3. _____
4. _____	4. _____
5. _____	5. _____
6. _____	6. _____
7. _____	7. _____

Prayer journal notes:

I Chronicles 28-29; John 9:24-41

_____

_____

_____

_____

_____

_____

_____

_____

DAY 147

Don't get discouraged if your plans fail. God's plan is what's best for you. He doesn't want you to have second best.

> *"Many are the plans in a man's heart, but it is the Lord's purpose that prevails."*
>
> Proverbs 19:21 NIV

PRAYER LIST	TO DO LIST
1. _____	1. _____
2. _____	2. _____
3. _____	3. _____
4. _____	4. _____
5. _____	5. _____
6. _____	6. _____
7. _____	7. _____

Prayer journal notes:

II Chronicles 1-3; John 10:1-23

_____

_____

_____

_____

_____

_____

_____

_____

_____

DAY 148

Don't allow any little god to come between you and Almighty God.

"No one can serve two masters. Either he will hate the one and love the other, or he will be devoted to the one and despise the other."

Matthew 6:24 NIV

PRAYER LIST	TO DO LIST
1. _____	1. _____
2. _____	2. _____
3. _____	3. _____
4. _____	4. _____
5. _____	5. _____
6. _____	6. _____
7. _____	7. _____

Prayer journal notes:

II Chronicles 4-6; John 10:24-42

_____
_____
_____
_____
_____
_____
_____
_____

DAY 149

The more we have seemed to have lost our way, the more we need to stop, be still, and listen.

"Be still and know that I am God."

Psalm 46:10 NIV

PRAYER LIST	TO DO LIST
1. _____	1. _____
2. _____	2. _____
3. _____	3. _____
4. _____	4. _____
5. _____	5. _____
6. _____	6. _____
7. _____	7. _____

Prayer journal notes:

II Chronicles 7-9; John 11:1-29

_____

_____

_____

_____

_____

_____

_____

_____

_____

_____

_____

DAY 150

When the storms rage, we often call on Jesus to bail water
— when He can remove the storm completely.

"Even the winds and waves obey Him."

Mark 4:41 NIV

PRAYER LIST	TO DO LIST
1. _____	1. _____
2. _____	2. _____
3. _____	3. _____
4. _____	4. _____
5. _____	5. _____
6. _____	6. _____
7. _____	7. _____

Prayer journal notes:

II Chronicles 10-12; John 11:30-57

_____
_____
_____
_____
_____
_____
_____
_____
_____
_____

DAY 151

Don't expect the harvest if you are not willing to plow.

"The harvest is plentiful but the workers are few."
Luke 10:2 NIV

PRAYER LIST	TO DO LIST
1. _____	1. _____
2. _____	2. _____
3. _____	3. _____
4. _____	4. _____
5. _____	5. _____
6. _____	6. _____
7. _____	7. _____

Prayer journal notes:

II Chronicles 13-14; John 12:1-26

_____

_____

_____

_____

_____

_____

_____

_____

_____

_____

DAY 152

Don't ask God to direct your steps if you are not willing to move your feet.

"He leads me beside the still waters."

Psalm 23:2 NIV

PRAYER LIST	TO DO LIST
1. _____	1. _____
2. _____	2. _____
3. _____	3. _____
4. _____	4. _____
5. _____	5. _____
6. _____	6. _____
7. _____	7. _____

Prayer journal notes:

II Chronicles 15-16; John 12:27-50

_____

_____

_____

_____

_____

_____

_____

_____

_____

_____

_____

DAY 153

We enjoy the freedoms we have because of those who were and are willing to die on our behalf.

> *"Greater love has no one than this, that he lay down his life for his friends."*
>
> *John 15:13 NIV*

PRAYER LIST	TO DO LIST
1. _____	1. _____
2. _____	2. _____
3. _____	3. _____
4. _____	4. _____
5. _____	5. _____
6. _____	6. _____
7. _____	7. _____

Prayer journal notes:

II Chronicles 17-18; John 13:1-20

_____

_____

_____

_____

_____

_____

_____

_____

DAY 154

When you totally rely on God, you always know from where you will get your second wind.

"He will keep you strong to the end."

1 Corinthians 1:8 NIV

PRAYER LIST	TO DO LIST
1. _____	1. _____
2. _____	2. _____
3. _____	3. _____
4. _____	4. _____
5. _____	5. _____
6. _____	6. _____
7. _____	7. _____

Prayer journal notes:

II Chronicles 19-20; John 13:21-38

_____

_____

_____

_____

_____

_____

_____

_____

_____

_____

_____

DAY 155

A gloomy Christian is a contradiction of terms. It's always a beautiful day regardless of the weather.

"Rejoice in the Lord always, again I say rejoice."
Philippians 4:4 NKJV

PRAYER LIST	TO DO LIST
1. _____	1. _____
2. _____	2. _____
3. _____	3. _____
4. _____	4. _____
5. _____	5. _____
6. _____	6. _____
7. _____	7. _____

Prayer journal notes:

II Chronicles 21-22; John 14

_____
_____
_____
_____
_____
_____
_____
_____
_____
_____

DAY 156

All hope is never lost when you believe in an all-powerful God. He spoke the world into existence; your problem is no problem.

> *"Where were you when I laid the foundation of the earth?"*
>
> *Job 38:4 NKJV*

PRAYER LIST	TO DO LIST
1. _____	1. _____
2. _____	2. _____
3. _____	3. _____
4. _____	4. _____
5. _____	5. _____
6. _____	6. _____
7. _____	7. _____

Prayer journal notes:

II Chronicles 23-24; John 15

_____

_____

_____

_____

_____

_____

_____

_____

DAY 157

God doesn't call us to be comfortable. He calls us to put our complete trust and faith in Him even when it is scary and doesn't make sense. What are you doing right now that requires total faith in God?

"So whether we live or die, we belong to the Lord."
Romans 14:8 NIV

PRAYER LIST	TO DO LIST
1. _____	1. _____
2. _____	2. _____
3. _____	3. _____
4. _____	4. _____
5. _____	5. _____
6. _____	6. _____
7. _____	7. _____

Prayer journal notes:

II Chronicles 25-27; John 16

_____
_____
_____
_____
_____
_____
_____
_____

DAY 158

Christians never say "good-bye" forever. Instead, it's "good-bye, until we meet again."

"We shall be caught up together with them in clouds."
1 Thessalonians 4:17 NKJV

PRAYER LIST

1. _____
2. _____
3. _____
4. _____
5. _____
6. _____
7. _____

TO DO LIST

1. _____
2. _____
3. _____
4. _____
5. _____
6. _____
7. _____

Prayer journal notes:

II Chronicles 28-29; John 17

_____
_____
_____
_____
_____
_____
_____
_____
_____
_____

DAY 159

You grow in spiritual maturity when your concern for others begins to outweigh your concern for yourself.

"Therefore let us leave the elementary teachings about Christ and go on to maturity..."

Hebrews 6:1 NIV

PRAYER LIST	TO DO LIST
1. _____	1. _____
2. _____	2. _____
3. _____	3. _____
4. _____	4. _____
5. _____	5. _____
6. _____	6. _____
7. _____	7. _____

Prayer journal notes:

II Chronicles 30-31; John 18:1-18

_____

_____

_____

_____

_____

_____

_____

_____

_____

DAY 160

There are many around the world that worship non-living gods. Pray that they will know that our God is God alone.

"O Lord our God, deliver us…so that all kingdoms on earth may know that You alone, O Lord, are God."

2 Kings 19:19 NIV

PRAYER LIST	TO DO LIST
1. _____	1. _____
2. _____	2. _____
3. _____	3. _____
4. _____	4. _____
5. _____	5. _____
6. _____	6. _____
7. _____	7. _____

Prayer journal notes:

II Chronicles 32-33; John 18:19-40

_____

_____

_____

_____

_____

_____

_____

_____

_____

DAY 161

Don't run away, meet your giant head on with reinforcements. Prayer is a support for everything you face today, not a substitute.

"…in everything, by prayer and petition, with thanksgiving, present your requests to God."

Philippians 4:6 NIV

PRAYER LIST	TO DO LIST
1. _____	1. _____
2. _____	2. _____
3. _____	3. _____
4. _____	4. _____
5. _____	5. _____
6. _____	6. _____
7. _____	7. _____

Prayer journal notes:

II Chronicles 34-36; John 19:1-22

_____

_____

_____

_____

_____

_____

_____

_____

DAY 162

You never have to worry about being taken care of if you spend your life taking care of others.

"The generous soul will be made rich, and he who waters will also be watered himself."

Proverbs 11:25 NKJV

PRAYER LIST	TO DO LIST
1. _____	1. _____
2. _____	2. _____
3. _____	3. _____
4. _____	4. _____
5. _____	5. _____
6. _____	6. _____
7. _____	7. _____

Prayer journal notes:

Ezra 1-2; John 19:23-42

_____

_____

_____

_____

_____

_____

_____

_____

_____

DAY 163

The biggest mistake that can be made as individuals or as a country is to no longer fear God.

> *"Fear the Lord your God, serve Him only...do not follow other gods...for the Lord is a jealous God...and He will destroy you from the face of the land."*
> *Deuteronomy 6:13-15 NIV*

PRAYER LIST	TO DO LIST
1. _____	1. _____
2. _____	2. _____
3. _____	3. _____
4. _____	4. _____
5. _____	5. _____
6. _____	6. _____
7. _____	7. _____

Prayer journal notes:

Ezra 3-5; John 20

_____
_____
_____
_____
_____
_____
_____
_____

DAY 164

Listen to your conscious. It is a built-in warning system that God provides. It's a good thing when it bothers you. It's a bad thing when it doesn't.

> *"So I strive always to keep my conscious clear before God and man."*
>
> Acts 24:16 NIV

PRAYER LIST	TO DO LIST
1. _____	1. _____
2. _____	2. _____
3. _____	3. _____
4. _____	4. _____
5. _____	5. _____
6. _____	6. _____
7. _____	7. _____

Prayer journal notes:

Ezra 6-8; John 21

_____

_____

_____

_____

_____

_____

_____

_____

DAY 165

You can be in a crowded room and still feel alone, but you are never alone. God is always there.

"I am with you always, even to the end of the age."
Matthew 28:20 NKJV

PRAYER LIST	TO DO LIST
1. _____	1. _____
2. _____	2. _____
3. _____	3. _____
4. _____	4. _____
5. _____	5. _____
6. _____	6. _____
7. _____	7. _____

Prayer journal notes:

Ezra 9-10; Acts 1

_____
_____
_____
_____
_____
_____
_____
_____
_____
_____

DAY 166

❧

Everyone sets an example for someone. What kind of example are you setting, and whose example are you following?

"Follow my example, as I follow the example of Christ."
1Corinthians 11:1 NIV

PRAYER LIST	TO DO LIST
1. _____	1. _____
2. _____	2. _____
3. _____	3. _____
4. _____	4. _____
5. _____	5. _____
6. _____	6. _____
7. _____	7. _____

Prayer journal notes:

Nehemiah 1-3; Acts 2:1-21

_____

_____

_____

_____

_____

_____

_____

_____

_____

_____

_____

DAY 167

Each day is a small part of the grindstone of life. Depending on what you are made of, it will either polish you up or grind you down.

"…and the fire will test the quality of each man's work."
1 Corinthians 3:13 NIV

PRAYER LIST	TO DO LIST
1. _____	1. _____
2. _____	2. _____
3. _____	3. _____
4. _____	4. _____
5. _____	5. _____
6. _____	6. _____
7. _____	7. _____

Prayer journal notes:

Nehemiah 4-6; Acts 2:22-47

_____

_____

_____

_____

_____

_____

_____

_____

_____

DAY 168

If you find yourself not as close to God as you once were, it wasn't God who slipped away. You are a prayer away from returning. You are as close to God as you choose to be.

"Draw near to God and He will draw near to you."

James 4:8 NKJV

PRAYER LIST	TO DO LIST
1. _____	1. _____
2. _____	2. _____
3. _____	3. _____
4. _____	4. _____
5. _____	5. _____
6. _____	6. _____
7. _____	7. _____

Prayer journal notes:

Nehemiah 7-9; Acts 3

_____

_____

_____

_____

_____

_____

_____

_____

_____

DAY 169

Always do right. What's right is right even if it seems no one is doing it. What's wrong is wrong even if it seems everyone is doing it. You can never go wrong doing what is right.

"And as for you brothers, never tire of doing what is right."
2 Thessalonians 3:13 NIV

PRAYER LIST	TO DO LIST
1. _____	1. _____
2. _____	2. _____
3. _____	3. _____
4. _____	4. _____
5. _____	5. _____
6. _____	6. _____
7. _____	7. _____

Prayer journal notes:

Nehemiah 10-11; Acts 4:1-22

_____

_____

_____

_____

_____

_____

_____

_____

DAY 170

Many times when praying, it's best to just stay quiet and listen to the ultimate authority of the universe.

"God is in heaven and you are on earth, so let your words be few."

Ecclesiastes 5:2 NIV

PRAYER LIST	TO DO LIST
1. _____	1. _____
2. _____	2. _____
3. _____	3. _____
4. _____	4. _____
5. _____	5. _____
6. _____	6. _____
7. _____	7. _____

Prayer journal notes:

Nehemiah 12-13; Acts 4:23-37

_____

_____

_____

_____

_____

_____

_____

_____

_____

_____

DAY 171

❦

The best gift for your father? Your time. Your presence will win out over your presents every time.

"A wise son brings joy to his father."

Proverbs 10:1 NIV

PRAYER LIST	TO DO LIST
1. _____	1. _____
2. _____	2. _____
3. _____	3. _____
4. _____	4. _____
5. _____	5. _____
6. _____	6. _____
7. _____	7. _____

Prayer journal notes:

Esther 1-2; Acts 5:1-21

_____
_____
_____
_____
_____
_____
_____
_____
_____
_____
_____

DAY 172

Even when you don't feel appreciated, you will never go wrong giving something your very best effort.

"Whatever you do, work at it with all your heart as if working for the Lord, not for men...it is the Lord Christ you are serving."

Colossians 3:23-25 NIV

PRAYER LIST	TO DO LIST
1. _____	1. _____
2. _____	2. _____
3. _____	3. _____
4. _____	4. _____
5. _____	5. _____
6. _____	6. _____
7. _____	7. _____

Prayer journal notes:

Esther 3-5; Acts 5:22-42

_____

_____

_____

_____

_____

_____

_____

_____

DAY 173

There are a lot of good things that are the result of honoring your father.

"Honor your father...that it may go well with you and that you may enjoy long life on the earth."

Ephesians 6:2-3 NIV

PRAYER LIST	TO DO LIST
1. _____	1. _____
2. _____	2. _____
3. _____	3. _____
4. _____	4. _____
5. _____	5. _____
6. _____	6. _____
7. _____	7. _____

Prayer journal notes:

Esther 6-8; Acts 6

_____

_____

_____

_____

_____

_____

_____

_____

DAY 174

As a Christian, what the world sees you are, they consider Christ to be. How's your walk?

"His command is that you walk in love."

2 John 6 NIV

PRAYER LIST	TO DO LIST
1. _____	1. _____
2. _____	2. _____
3. _____	3. _____
4. _____	4. _____
5. _____	5. _____
6. _____	6. _____
7. _____	7. _____

Prayer journal notes:

Esther 9-10; Acts 7:1-21

_____
_____
_____
_____
_____
_____
_____
_____
_____
_____
_____

DAY 175

꩜

With God in your life, bad days are few. It is better to have a bad day with God than a good day without Him.

"Better is one day in Your courts than a thousand elsewhere."

Psalm 84:10 NIV

PRAYER LIST	TO DO LIST
1. _____	1. _____
2. _____	2. _____
3. _____	3. _____
4. _____	4. _____
5. _____	5. _____
6. _____	6. _____
7. _____	7. _____

Prayer journal notes:

Job 1-2; Acts 7:22-43

_____

_____

_____

_____

_____

_____

_____

_____

_____

DAY 176

Our self-worth is found in the fact that Almighty God loves us unconditionally. What we have or don't have that is measured by the world means nothing.

> *"This is real love; not that we loved God but that He loved us."*
>
> 1 John 4:10 NIV

PRAYER LIST	TO DO LIST
1. _____	1. _____
2. _____	2. _____
3. _____	3. _____
4. _____	4. _____
5. _____	5. _____
6. _____	6. _____
7. _____	7. _____

Prayer journal notes:

Job 3-4; Acts 7:44-60

_____
_____
_____
_____
_____
_____
_____
_____

DAY 177

Servant leadership is a hot topic in our world today, and it should be. It originated with the greatest servant leader ever.

> *"For the Son of Man did not come to be served, but to serve."*
>
> *Mark 10:45 NIV*

PRAYER LIST	TO DO LIST
1. _____	1. _____
2. _____	2. _____
3. _____	3. _____
4. _____	4. _____
5. _____	5. _____
6. _____	6. _____
7. _____	7. _____

Prayer journal notes:

Job 5-7; Acts 8:1-25

_____

_____

_____

_____

_____

_____

_____

_____

_____

DAY 178

Our limitations never limit God. When we are weak, He is strong.

> *"My grace is sufficient for you, for My power is made perfect in weakness...for when I am weak, then I am strong."*
>
> *2 Corinthians 12:9-10 NIV*

PRAYER LIST	TO DO LIST
1. _____	1. _____
2. _____	2. _____
3. _____	3. _____
4. _____	4. _____
5. _____	5. _____
6. _____	6. _____
7. _____	7. _____

Prayer journal notes:

Job 8-10; Acts 8:26-40

_____
_____
_____
_____
_____
_____
_____
_____

DAY 179

The measure of a man is not what he has, but what he has given.

> *"Command them to do good, to be rich in good deeds, and to be generous and willing to share."*
>
> 1 Timothy 6:18 NIV

PRAYER LIST	TO DO LIST
1. _____	1. _____
2. _____	2. _____
3. _____	3. _____
4. _____	4. _____
5. _____	5. _____
6. _____	6. _____
7. _____	7. _____

Prayer journal notes:

Job 11-13; Acts 9:1-21

_____

_____

_____

_____

_____

_____

_____

_____

_____

DAY 180

There is no need to fear the battle...the victory is already His.

"Be strong in the Lord and in His mighty power."
Ephesians 6:10 NIV

PRAYER LIST	TO DO LIST
1. _____	1. _____
2. _____	2. _____
3. _____	3. _____
4. _____	4. _____
5. _____	5. _____
6. _____	6. _____
7. _____	7. _____

Prayer journal notes:

Job 14-16; Acts 9:22-43

_____
_____
_____
_____
_____
_____
_____
_____
_____
_____
_____
_____

DAY 181

When you get a good feeling and you don't know why, there is a good chance someone who loves you is praying for you and God is about to pour out His blessings upon you because of them.

"I have learned by experience that the Lord has blessed me because of you."

Genesis 30:27 NKJV

PRAYER LIST	TO DO LIST
1. _____	1. _____
2. _____	2. _____
3. _____	3. _____
4. _____	4. _____
5. _____	5. _____
6. _____	6. _____
7. _____	7. _____

Prayer journal notes:

Job 17-19; Acts 10:1-23

_____

_____

_____

_____

_____

_____

_____

DAY 182

In a world where it is hard to believe anything you hear or read, you never have to doubt what God says.

"I, the Lord, speak the truth. I declare what is right."
Isaiah 45:19 NIV

PRAYER LIST	TO DO LIST
1. _____	1. _____
2. _____	2. _____
3. _____	3. _____
4. _____	4. _____
5. _____	5. _____
6. _____	6. _____
7. _____	7. _____

Prayer journal notes:

Job 20-21; Acts 10:24-48

_____
_____
_____
_____
_____
_____
_____
_____
_____
_____
_____

DAY 183

Whatever you are fighting today, fight with confidence. You are an overcomer by the blood of the Lamb.

"They overcame him by the blood of the Lamb."
Revelation 12:11 NIV

PRAYER LIST	TO DO LIST
1. _____	1. _____
2. _____	2. _____
3. _____	3. _____
4. _____	4. _____
5. _____	5. _____
6. _____	6. _____
7. _____	7. _____

Prayer journal notes:

Job 22-24; Acts 11

_____

_____

_____

_____

_____

_____

_____

_____

_____

DAY 184

The secret to staying afloat financially is to make sure your earnings always exceed your yearnings.

"Keep your lives free from the love of money and be content with what you have."

Hebrews 13:5 NIV

PRAYER LIST	TO DO LIST
1. _____	1. _____
2. _____	2. _____
3. _____	3. _____
4. _____	4. _____
5. _____	5. _____
6. _____	6. _____
7. _____	7. _____

Prayer journal notes:

Job 25-27; Acts 12

_____

_____

_____

_____

_____

_____

_____

_____

_____

DAY 185

It is smarter to turn to God on your own than to wait for Him to get your attention.

"From on high He sent fire, sent it down into my bones."
Lamentations 1:13 NIV

PRAYER LIST	TO DO LIST
1. _____	1. _____
2. _____	2. _____
3. _____	3. _____
4. _____	4. _____
5. _____	5. _____
6. _____	6. _____
7. _____	7. _____

Prayer journal notes:

Job 28-29; Acts 13:1-25

_____
_____
_____
_____
_____
_____
_____
_____
_____
_____

DAY 186

Shine your light today in such a way that everyone around you is so positively impacted that they ask you about the originator of the light.

"Let your light so shine before men, that they may see your good works and glorify your Father in heaven."
Matthew 5:16 NKJV

PRAYER LIST	TO DO LIST
1. _____	1. _____
2. _____	2. _____
3. _____	3. _____
4. _____	4. _____
5. _____	5. _____
6. _____	6. _____
7. _____	7. _____

Prayer journal notes:

Job 30-31; Acts 13:26-52

_____
_____
_____
_____
_____
_____
_____
_____

DAY 187

God blesses those who are humble, obedient, and follow His commands. May our nation always be blessed.

"Blessed is the nation whose God is the Lord."
Psalm 33:12 NIV

PRAYER LIST	TO DO LIST
1. _____	1. _____
2. _____	2. _____
3. _____	3. _____
4. _____	4. _____
5. _____	5. _____
6. _____	6. _____
7. _____	7. _____

Prayer journal notes:

Job 32-33; Acts 14

_____
_____
_____
_____
_____
_____
_____
_____
_____
_____

DAY 188

God doesn't expect us to understand Him, but to trust Him.
God is great, God is good, but not all He does is understood.

> *"God's voice thunders…He does great things beyond our understanding."*
>
> *Job 37:5 NIV*

PRAYER LIST	TO DO LIST
1. _____	1. _____
2. _____	2. _____
3. _____	3. _____
4. _____	4. _____
5. _____	5. _____
6. _____	6. _____
7. _____	7. _____

Prayer journal notes:

Job 34-35; Acts 15:1-21

_____

_____

_____

_____

_____

_____

_____

_____

_____

DAY 189

Be comforted today in the security of God.
A benefit of being in the royal family of God is that secret service is provided.

"Lord you are all I want! You are my choice and You keep me safe."

Psalm 16:5 CEV

PRAYER LIST	TO DO LIST
1. _____	1. _____
2. _____	2. _____
3. _____	3. _____
4. _____	4. _____
5. _____	5. _____
6. _____	6. _____
7. _____	7. _____

Prayer journal notes:

Job 36-37; Acts 15:22-41

_____
_____
_____
_____
_____
_____
_____
_____

DAY 190

If we never receive another blessing, God has blessed us more than we deserve.

"The Lord is good to all; He has compassion on all He has made."

Psalm 145:9 NIV

PRAYER LIST	TO DO LIST
1. _____	1. _____
2. _____	2. _____
3. _____	3. _____
4. _____	4. _____
5. _____	5. _____
6. _____	6. _____
7. _____	7. _____

Prayer journal notes:

Job 38-40; Acts 16:1-21

_____

_____

_____

_____

_____

_____

_____

_____

_____

DAY 191

❧

You reap what you sow, and that includes in business.

"The wicked man earns deceptive wages, but he who sows righteousness reaps a sure reward."

Proverbs 11:18 NIV

PRAYER LIST	TO DO LIST
1. _____	1. _____
2. _____	2. _____
3. _____	3. _____
4. _____	4. _____
5. _____	5. _____
6. _____	6. _____
7. _____	7. _____

Prayer journal notes:

Job 41-42; Acts 16:22-40

_____
_____
_____
_____
_____
_____
_____
_____
_____
_____
_____

DAY 192

The best things in life aren't things. We are rich regardless of our material possessions.

"Those who seek the Lord lack no good thing."
Psalm 34:10 NIV

PRAYER LIST	TO DO LIST
1. _____	1. _____
2. _____	2. _____
3. _____	3. _____
4. _____	4. _____
5. _____	5. _____
6. _____	6. _____
7. _____	7. _____

Prayer journal notes:

Psalms 1-3; Acts 17:1-15

_____
_____
_____
_____
_____
_____
_____
_____
_____
_____
_____

DAY 193

Our greatest success occurs and continues when we recognize and acknowledge from where our ability to be successful comes.

> *"But remember the Lord your God, for it is He who gives you the ability to produce wealth..."*
>
> *Deuteronomy 8:18 NIV*

PRAYER LIST	TO DO LIST
1. _____	1. _____
2. _____	2. _____
3. _____	3. _____
4. _____	4. _____
5. _____	5. _____
6. _____	6. _____
7. _____	7. _____

Prayer journal notes:

Psalms 4-6; Acts 17:16-34

_____

_____

_____

_____

_____

_____

_____

_____

DAY 194

Fruit bearers have to stay connected to their source of nourishment.

"I am the vine; you are the branches. If a man remains in Me and I in him, he will bear much fruit; apart from Me you can do nothing."

John 15:5 NIV

PRAYER LIST	TO DO LIST
1. _____	1. _____
2. _____	2. _____
3. _____	3. _____
4. _____	4. _____
5. _____	5. _____
6. _____	6. _____
7. _____	7. _____

Prayer journal notes:

Psalms 7-9; Acts 18

_____

_____

_____

_____

_____

_____

_____

_____

DAY 195

We are to encourage, not discourage. We can be either a stepping stone or a stumbling block for others. Which are you?

"Do not cause anyone to stumble..."

1 Corinthians 10:32 NIV

PRAYER LIST	TO DO LIST
1. _____	1. _____
2. _____	2. _____
3. _____	3. _____
4. _____	4. _____
5. _____	5. _____
6. _____	6. _____
7. _____	7. _____

Prayer journal notes:

Psalms 10-12; Acts 19:1-20

_____

_____

_____

_____

_____

_____

_____

_____

DAY 196

Prayer is not pulling God to our plan, but the aligning of ourselves to His plan.

"...Our Father in heaven...Your kingdom come, Your will be done..."

Matthew 6:9-10 NIV

PRAYER LIST	TO DO LIST
1. _____	1. _____
2. _____	2. _____
3. _____	3. _____
4. _____	4. _____
5. _____	5. _____
6. _____	6. _____
7. _____	7. _____

Prayer journal notes:

Psalms 13-15; Acts 19:21-41

_____

_____

_____

_____

_____

_____

_____

_____

_____

DAY 197

Be careful what you take to heart. If it comes from man, make sure that it is God-inspired. Therefore put your trust in Christ, not man.

"I am the way, the truth, and the life."

John 14:6 NIV

PRAYER LIST

1. _____
2. _____
3. _____
4. _____
5. _____
6. _____
7. _____

TO DO LIST

1. _____
2. _____
3. _____
4. _____
5. _____
6. _____
7. _____

Prayer journal notes:

Psalms 16-17; Acts 20:1-16

_____

_____

_____

_____

_____

_____

_____

_____

DAY 198

It has been said that heaven has a room filled with blessings that you did not receive on earth because you never asked for them.

"You do not have because you do not ask God."

James 4:2 NIV

PRAYER LIST	TO DO LIST
1. _____	1. _____
2. _____	2. _____
3. _____	3. _____
4. _____	4. _____
5. _____	5. _____
6. _____	6. _____
7. _____	7. _____

Prayer journal notes:

Psalms 18-19; Acts 20:17-38

_____

_____

_____

_____

_____

_____

_____

_____

_____

DAY 199

God wants your availability much more than your ability. God doesn't just call those who are qualified, He qualifies those He calls.

"...giving thanks to the Father, who has qualified you."
Colossians 1:12 NIV

PRAYER LIST	TO DO LIST
1. _____	1. _____
2. _____	2. _____
3. _____	3. _____
4. _____	4. _____
5. _____	5. _____
6. _____	6. _____
7. _____	7. _____

Prayer journal notes:

Psalms 20-22; Acts 21:1-17

_____

_____

_____

_____

_____

_____

_____

_____

_____

DAY 200

It is wise to listen to the wise if they are Godly-wise and tell you what you need to hear versus what you want to hear.

"It is better to heed a wise man's rebuke than to listen to the song of fools."

Ecclesiastes 7:5 NIV

PRAYER LIST	TO DO LIST
1. _____	1. _____
2. _____	2. _____
3. _____	3. _____
4. _____	4. _____
5. _____	5. _____
6. _____	6. _____
7. _____	7. _____

Prayer journal notes:

Psalms 23-25; Acts 21:18-40

_____

_____

_____

_____

_____

_____

_____

_____

_____

DAY 201

Patience is a virtue. Patience has been defined as having the ability to idle your engine when you are ready and able to put the petal to the metal.

"Be completely humble and gentle; be patient, bearing with one another in love."

Ephesians 4:2 NIV

PRAYER LIST	TO DO LIST
1. _____	1. _____
2. _____	2. _____
3. _____	3. _____
4. _____	4. _____
5. _____	5. _____
6. _____	6. _____
7. _____	7. _____

Prayer journal notes:

Psalms 26-28; Acts 22

_____

_____

_____

_____

_____

_____

_____

_____

DAY 202

We will only have a faith that is triumphal when it has been battle tested.

"Consider it pure joy, my brothers, whenever you face trials of many kinds, because you know that the testing of your faith develops perseverance."

James 1:2-3 NIV

PRAYER LIST	TO DO LIST
1. _____	1. _____
2. _____	2. _____
3. _____	3. _____
4. _____	4. _____
5. _____	5. _____
6. _____	6. _____
7. _____	7. _____

Prayer journal notes:

Psalms 29-30; Acts 23:1-15

_____
_____
_____
_____
_____
_____
_____
_____
_____

DAY 203

Faith really grows where you and God goes.

"But when you pray, go into your room, close the door and pray to your Father, who is unseen. Then your Father, who sees what is done in secret, will reward you."
Matthew 6:6 NIV

PRAYER LIST	TO DO LIST
1. _____	1. _____
2. _____	2. _____
3. _____	3. _____
4. _____	4. _____
5. _____	5. _____
6. _____	6. _____
7. _____	7. _____

Prayer journal notes:

Psalms 31-32; Acts 23:16-35

_____

_____

_____

_____

_____

_____

_____

_____

_____

DAY 204

All of our tomorrows are with God; safe and secure.

"So don't be anxious about tomorrow. God will take care of your tomorrow too. Live one day at a time."

Matthew 6:34 TLB

PRAYER LIST	TO DO LIST
1. _____	1. _____
2. _____	2. _____
3. _____	3. _____
4. _____	4. _____
5. _____	5. _____
6. _____	6. _____
7. _____	7. _____

Prayer journal notes:

Psalms 33-34; Acts 24

_____

_____

_____

_____

_____

_____

_____

_____

_____

_____

_____

DAY 205

Remember to distinguish between your wants and your needs. You have a loving Heavenly Father who will provide all your needs today.

"Your Father knows the things you have need of before you ask Him."

Matthew 6:8 NKJV

PRAYER LIST	TO DO LIST
1. _____	1. _____
2. _____	2. _____
3. _____	3. _____
4. _____	4. _____
5. _____	5. _____
6. _____	6. _____
7. _____	7. _____

Prayer journal notes:

Psalms 35-36; Acts 25

_____

_____

_____

_____

_____

_____

_____

_____

DAY 206

God gives us peace like a baby sleeping.

> *"I will lie down and sleep in peace, for you alone, O Lord, make me dwell in safety."*
>
> *Psalm 4:8 NIV*

PRAYER LIST	TO DO LIST
1. _____	1. _____
2. _____	2. _____
3. _____	3. _____
4. _____	4. _____
5. _____	5. _____
6. _____	6. _____
7. _____	7. _____

Prayer journal notes:

Psalms 37-39; Acts 26

_____

_____

_____

_____

_____

_____

_____

_____

_____

_____

DAY 207

United we stand. Divided we fall. We were created to be interdependent, not independent. We are much better when we work together.

> "From Him the whole body, joined and held together by every supporting ligament, grows and builds itself up in love, as each part does its work."
>
> *Ephesians 4:16 NIV*

PRAYER LIST	TO DO LIST
1. _____	1. _____
2. _____	2. _____
3. _____	3. _____
4. _____	4. _____
5. _____	5. _____
6. _____	6. _____
7. _____	7. _____

Prayer journal notes:

Psalms 40-42; Acts 27:1-26

_____
_____
_____
_____
_____
_____
_____
_____

DAY 208

There will be times when we don't feel like praying. Those are the times when we need to pray the most.

"The Spirit helps us in our weakness. We do not know what we ought to pray for, but the Spirit Himself intercedes for us."

Romans 8:26 NIV

PRAYER LIST	TO DO LIST
1. _____	1. _____
2. _____	2. _____
3. _____	3. _____
4. _____	4. _____
5. _____	5. _____
6. _____	6. _____
7. _____	7. _____

Prayer journal notes:

Psalms 43-45; Acts 27:27-44

_____

_____

_____

_____

_____

_____

_____

_____

DAY 209

Success is not an entry level job. We are better when we've had to work for and wait on success.

> *"The end of a matter is better than its beginning, and patience is better than pride."*
>
> Ecclesiastes 7:8 NIV

PRAYER LIST	TO DO LIST
1. _____	1. _____
2. _____	2. _____
3. _____	3. _____
4. _____	4. _____
5. _____	5. _____
6. _____	6. _____
7. _____	7. _____

Prayer journal notes:

Psalms 46-48; Acts 28

_____
_____
_____
_____
_____
_____
_____
_____
_____

DAY 210

There are but a few things in life that you can truly, always, beyond a shadow of a doubt count on.

> *"Jesus Christ is the same yesterday and today and forever."*
>
> Hebrews 13:8 NIV

PRAYER LIST	TO DO LIST
1. _____	1. _____
2. _____	2. _____
3. _____	3. _____
4. _____	4. _____
5. _____	5. _____
6. _____	6. _____
7. _____	7. _____

Prayer journal notes:

Psalms 49-50; Romans 1

_____
_____
_____
_____
_____
_____
_____
_____
_____
_____

DAY 211

Your candle doesn't go out when you light someone else's. The light just grows stronger. The only thing we really keep in this life is what we give away.

"Every man shall give as he is able, according to the blessing of the Lord your God which He has given you."
Deuteronomy 16:17 NKJV

PRAYER LIST	TO DO LIST
1. _____	1. _____
2. _____	2. _____
3. _____	3. _____
4. _____	4. _____
5. _____	5. _____
6. _____	6. _____
7. _____	7. _____

Prayer journal notes:

Psalms 51-53; Romans 2

_____

_____

_____

_____

_____

_____

_____

_____

DAY 212

With your adoption into the family of God comes a guarantee unlike any other.

"Now it is God who has made us…and has given us the Spirit as a deposit, guaranteeing what is to come."
2 Corinthians 5:5 NIV

PRAYER LIST	TO DO LIST
1. _____	1. _____
2. _____	2. _____
3. _____	3. _____
4. _____	4. _____
5. _____	5. _____
6. _____	6. _____
7. _____	7. _____

Prayer journal notes:

Psalms 54-56; Romans 3

_____

_____

_____

_____

_____

_____

_____

_____

_____

DAY 213

Don't save anything for a special occasion in the future. God waking you up this morning and being alive today is a special occasion.

"We have seen remarkable things today."

Luke 5:6 NLT

PRAYER LIST	TO DO LIST
1. _____	1. _____
2. _____	2. _____
3. _____	3. _____
4. _____	4. _____
5. _____	5. _____
6. _____	6. _____
7. _____	7. _____

Prayer journal notes:

Psalms 57-59; Romans 4

_____

_____

_____

_____

_____

_____

_____

_____

DAY 214

May others see you today as proof that God is alive and loves them.

"Whoever lives in love lives in God, and God in him."
1 John 4:16 NIV

PRAYER LIST	TO DO LIST
1. _____	1. _____
2. _____	2. _____
3. _____	3. _____
4. _____	4. _____
5. _____	5. _____
6. _____	6. _____
7. _____	7. _____

Prayer journal notes:

Psalms 60-62; Romans 5

_____

_____

_____

_____

_____

_____

_____

_____

_____

_____

DAY 215

Regardless of how negative things may be, a Christian always has something to look forward to.

"I consider that our present sufferings are not worth comparing with the glory that will be revealed in us."

Romans 8:18 NIV

PRAYER LIST	TO DO LIST
1. _____	1. _____
2. _____	2. _____
3. _____	3. _____
4. _____	4. _____
5. _____	5. _____
6. _____	6. _____
7. _____	7. _____

Prayer journal notes:

Psalms 63-65; Romans 6

_____

_____

_____

_____

_____

_____

_____

_____

_____

DAY 216

If you truly love someone, you show them. Love is like faith, without action, it is dead.

*"Dear children, let us not merely say we love each other;
let us show it by our actions."*

1 John 3:18 NLT

PRAYER LIST	TO DO LIST
1. _____	1. _____
2. _____	2. _____
3. _____	3. _____
4. _____	4. _____
5. _____	5. _____
6. _____	6. _____
7. _____	7. _____

Prayer journal notes:

Psalms 66-67; Romans 7

_____

_____

_____

_____

_____

_____

_____

_____

_____

_____

DAY 217

In every situation, we have two choices and one best option.
Trust in the Lord, or choose option number two.

> *"Some trust in chariots and some in horses, but we trust
> in the name of the Lord our God."*
>
> Psalm 20:7 NIV

PRAYER LIST	TO DO LIST
1. _____	1. _____
2. _____	2. _____
3. _____	3. _____
4. _____	4. _____
5. _____	5. _____
6. _____	6. _____
7. _____	7. _____

Prayer journal notes:

Psalms 68-69; Romans 8:1-21

_____

_____

_____

_____

_____

_____

_____

_____

DAY 218

Don't be so busy adding up your troubles that you forget to count your blessings.

"Lord I remember what You have done. I remember the amazing things You did long ago. I think about them all the time."

Psalm 77:11-12 ERV

PRAYER LIST	TO DO LIST
1. _____	1. _____
2. _____	2. _____
3. _____	3. _____
4. _____	4. _____
5. _____	5. _____
6. _____	6. _____
7. _____	7. _____

Prayer journal notes:

Psalms 70-71; Romans 8:22-39

_____

_____

_____

_____

_____

_____

_____

_____

DAY 219

When things aren't going your way, remember it's not the outlook, but where you look that matters.

> "Looking unto Jesus, the author and finisher of our faith..."
>
> Hebrews 12:2 MEV

PRAYER LIST	TO DO LIST
1. _____	1. _____
2. _____	2. _____
3. _____	3. _____
4. _____	4. _____
5. _____	5. _____
6. _____	6. _____
7. _____	7. _____

Prayer journal notes:

Psalms 72-73; Romans 9:1-15

_____

_____

_____

_____

_____

_____

_____

_____

DAY 220

Good intentions never substitute for taking action. Don't miss a blessing by allowing your wishbone to be where your backbone should have been.

"Be strong and courageous…do not be discouraged, for the Lord your God will be with you wherever you go."

Joshua 1:9 NIV

PRAYER LIST	TO DO LIST
1. _____	1. _____
2. _____	2. _____
3. _____	3. _____
4. _____	4. _____
5. _____	5. _____
6. _____	6. _____
7. _____	7. _____

Prayer journal notes:

Psalms 74-76; Romans 9:16-33

_____

_____

_____

_____

_____

_____

_____

_____

DAY 221

⌒

When God is for you, it doesn't matter who is against you.

*"When I cry out to You, then my enemies will turn back;
this I know, because God is for me."*

Psalm 56:9 NKJV

PRAYER LIST	TO DO LIST
1. _____	1. _____
2. _____	2. _____
3. _____	3. _____
4. _____	4. _____
5. _____	5. _____
6. _____	6. _____
7. _____	7. _____

Prayer journal notes:

Psalms 77-78; Romans 10

_____

_____

_____

_____

_____

_____

_____

_____

_____

_____

_____

DAY 222

Never think doing the right thing is not the right thing to do. Payday is coming. The harvest can only be as productive as what was planted.

"So let us not grow weary in doing what is right, for we will reap at harvest time if we do not give up."
Galatians 6:9 NRSV

PRAYER LIST	TO DO LIST
1. _____	1. _____
2. _____	2. _____
3. _____	3. _____
4. _____	4. _____
5. _____	5. _____
6. _____	6. _____
7. _____	7. _____

Prayer journal notes:

Psalms 79-80; Romans 11:1-18

_____
_____
_____
_____
_____
_____
_____
_____

DAY 223

It is to our advantage to be able to not only work harder, but to work smarter.

"The work of God is this: to believe in the One He has sent."
John 6:29 NIV

PRAYER LIST	TO DO LIST
1. _____	1. _____
2. _____	2. _____
3. _____	3. _____
4. _____	4. _____
5. _____	5. _____
6. _____	6. _____
7. _____	7. _____

Prayer journal notes:

Psalms 81-83; Romans 11:19-36

_____

_____

_____

_____

_____

_____

_____

_____

_____

_____

DAY 224

〜✺

Even at the point where God is all you have left; you have everything you need.

"…and I will dwell in the house of the Lord forever."
Psalm 23:6 NIV

PRAYER LIST	TO DO LIST
1. _____	1. _____
2. _____	2. _____
3. _____	3. _____
4. _____	4. _____
5. _____	5. _____
6. _____	6. _____
7. _____	7. _____

Prayer journal notes:

Psalms 84-86; Romans 12

_____

_____

_____

_____

_____

_____

_____

_____

_____

_____

DAY 225

Never underestimate the power of prayer. When we work, we work. When we pray, God works.

"The prayer of a righteous man is powerful and effective."
James 5:16 NIV

PRAYER LIST	TO DO LIST
1. _____	1. _____
2. _____	2. _____
3. _____	3. _____
4. _____	4. _____
5. _____	5. _____
6. _____	6. _____
7. _____	7. _____

Prayer journal notes:

Psalms 87-88; Romans 13

_____
_____
_____
_____
_____
_____
_____
_____
_____
_____

DAY 226

You become like those you spend the most time with. Spend time with those who make you better.

"Dear children, do not let anyone lead you astray."
1 John 3:7 NIV

PRAYER LIST	TO DO LIST
1. _____	1. _____
2. _____	2. _____
3. _____	3. _____
4. _____	4. _____
5. _____	5. _____
6. _____	6. _____
7. _____	7. _____

Prayer journal notes:

Psalms 89-90; Romans 14

_____
_____
_____
_____
_____
_____
_____
_____
_____
_____
_____

DAY 227

Don't worry about those who give you trouble. Smile and move on. You have connections. God has your back.

"God is just: He will pay back trouble to those who trouble you."

2 Thessalonians 1:6 NIV

PRAYER LIST	TO DO LIST
1. _____	1. _____
2. _____	2. _____
3. _____	3. _____
4. _____	4. _____
5. _____	5. _____
6. _____	6. _____
7. _____	7. _____

Prayer journal notes:

Psalms 91-93; Romans 15:1-13

_____

_____

_____

_____

_____

_____

_____

_____

_____

DAY 228

Never forget where your success and accomplishments come from. If you do, He may remind you.

"Unless the Lord builds the house, its builders labor in vain."
Psalm 127:1 NIV

PRAYER LIST	TO DO LIST
1. _____	1. _____
2. _____	2. _____
3. _____	3. _____
4. _____	4. _____
5. _____	5. _____
6. _____	6. _____
7. _____	7. _____

Prayer journal notes:

Psalms 94-96; Romans 15:14-33

_____
_____
_____
_____
_____
_____
_____
_____
_____
_____
_____

DAY 229

Make wise choices. What and where you will be tomorrow
depends on the choices you make today.

*"How much better to get wisdom than gold, to choose
understanding rather than silver."*

Proverbs 16:16 NIV

PRAYER LIST	TO DO LIST
1. _____	1. _____
2. _____	2. _____
3. _____	3. _____
4. _____	4. _____
5. _____	5. _____
6. _____	6. _____
7. _____	7. _____

Prayer journal notes:

Psalms 97-99; Romans 16

_____

_____

_____

_____

_____

_____

_____

_____

_____

DAY 230

You may be the only lighthouse in someone else's storm.
Don't let them down. Shine brightly and lead them to shore.

"For God, who said, 'Let light shine out of darkness,'
made His light shine in our hearts..."

2 Corinthians 4:6 NIV

PRAYER LIST	TO DO LIST
1. _____	1. _____
2. _____	2. _____
3. _____	3. _____
4. _____	4. _____
5. _____	5. _____
6. _____	6. _____
7. _____	7. _____

Prayer journal notes:

Psalms 100-102; I Corinthians 1

_____

_____

_____

_____

_____

_____

_____

_____

_____

DAY 231

You were created to be like an eagle at heart. Don't settle for staying on the perch. You are equipped to soar.

> *"But those who hope in the Lord will renew their strength. They will soar on wings like eagles; they will run and not grow weary, they will walk and not be faint."*
>
> *Isaiah 40:31 NIV*

PRAYER LIST	TO DO LIST
1. _____	1. _____
2. _____	2. _____
3. _____	3. _____
4. _____	4. _____
5. _____	5. _____
6. _____	6. _____
7. _____	7. _____

Prayer journal notes:

Psalms 103-104; I Corinthians 2

_____

_____

_____

_____

_____

_____

_____

_____

DAY 232

Great things are coming on the road up ahead if you just keep walking.

> *"'For I know the plans I have for you,' declares the Lord, 'plans to prosper you...plans to give you a hope and a future.'"*
>
> Jeremiah 29:11 NIV

PRAYER LIST	TO DO LIST
1. _____	1. _____
2. _____	2. _____
3. _____	3. _____
4. _____	4. _____
5. _____	5. _____
6. _____	6. _____
7. _____	7. _____

Prayer journal notes:

Psalms 105-106; I Corinthians 3

_____

_____

_____

_____

_____

_____

_____

_____

DAY 233

We will never be called to serve God as a spiritual hermit on a deserted island. We are a part of a family that must work together.

"So in Christ we who are many form one body, and each member belongs to all the others."

Romans 12:5 NIV

PRAYER LIST	TO DO LIST
1. _____	1. _____
2. _____	2. _____
3. _____	3. _____
4. _____	4. _____
5. _____	5. _____
6. _____	6. _____
7. _____	7. _____

Prayer journal notes:

Psalms 107-109; I Corinthians 4

_____
_____
_____
_____
_____
_____
_____
_____

DAY 234

You can take your trials and temptations to Jesus. He understands them all.

> *"For we do not have a high priest who is unable to empathize with our weaknesses, but we have One who has been tempted in every way, just as we are -- yet he did not sin."*
>
> *Hebrews 4:15 NIV*

PRAYER LIST	TO DO LIST
1. _____	1. _____
2. _____	2. _____
3. _____	3. _____
4. _____	4. _____
5. _____	5. _____
6. _____	6. _____
7. _____	7. _____

Prayer journal notes:

Psalms 110-112; I Corinthians 5

_____

_____

_____

_____

_____

_____

_____

_____

DAY 235

God wants to be personally involved in the day to day details of your life. Nothing is too small. If it concerns you, it concerns Him.

"All the days ordained for me were written in Your book before one of them came to be."

Psalm 139:16 NIV

PRAYER LIST	TO DO LIST
1. _____	1. _____
2. _____	2. _____
3. _____	3. _____
4. _____	4. _____
5. _____	5. _____
6. _____	6. _____
7. _____	7. _____

Prayer journal notes:

Psalms 113-115; I Corinthians 6

_____

_____

_____

_____

_____

_____

_____

_____

DAY 236

There is a direct relationship between your amount of faith and the amount of time you spend in the Word.

"So then faith comes by hearing, and hearing by the Word of God…"

Romans 10:17 NKJV

PRAYER LIST	TO DO LIST
1. _____	1. _____
2. _____	2. _____
3. _____	3. _____
4. _____	4. _____
5. _____	5. _____
6. _____	6. _____
7. _____	7. _____

Prayer journal notes:

Psalms 116-118; I Corinthians 7:1-19

_____

_____

_____

_____

_____

_____

_____

_____

DAY 237

You will never hit a home run if you are afraid of striking out. Those who accomplish great things are usually those who were unsuccessful several times before.

"But let patience have its perfect work, that you may be perfect and complete, lacking nothing."

James 1:4 NKJV

PRAYER LIST	TO DO LIST
1. _____	1. _____
2. _____	2. _____
3. _____	3. _____
4. _____	4. _____
5. _____	5. _____
6. _____	6. _____
7. _____	7. _____

Prayer journal notes:

Psalms 119:1-88; I Corinthians 7:20-40

_____
_____
_____
_____
_____
_____
_____
_____

DAY 238

For every mile of road, there are two miles of ditches. Stay focused. Don't allow anything to distract you from staying on the road.

> *"Let your eyes look straight ahead, fix your gaze directly before you. Make level paths for your feet and take only ways that are firm. Do not swerve to the right or the left."*
>
> Proverbs 4:25-27 NIV

PRAYER LIST	TO DO LIST
1. _____	1. _____
2. _____	2. _____
3. _____	3. _____
4. _____	4. _____
5. _____	5. _____
6. _____	6. _____
7. _____	7. _____

Prayer journal notes:

Psalms 119:89-176; I Corinthians 8

_____

_____

_____

_____

_____

_____

_____

_____

_____

DAY 239

Kindness acts as the oil that takes the friction out of life. It is a double positive. It can change both the giver and receiver for the better.

"But the fruit if the spirit is...kindness."

Galatians 5:22 NIV

PRAYER LIST	TO DO LIST
1. _____	1. _____
2. _____	2. _____
3. _____	3. _____
4. _____	4. _____
5. _____	5. _____
6. _____	6. _____
7. _____	7. _____

Prayer journal notes:

Psalms 120-122; I Corinthians 9

_____

_____

_____

_____

_____

_____

_____

_____

DAY 240

There will come a day when God will put an end to all our troubles. Until then, may we find peace in His presence.

"I have told you these things, so that in Me you may have peace. In this world you will have trouble. But take heart! I have overcome the world."

John 16:33 NIV

PRAYER LIST

1. _____
2. _____
3. _____
4. _____
5. _____
6. _____
7. _____

TO DO LIST

1. _____
2. _____
3. _____
4. _____
5. _____
6. _____
7. _____

Prayer journal notes:

Psalms 123-125; I Corinthians 10:1-18

_____
_____
_____
_____
_____
_____
_____
_____

DAY 241

Christianity is not a spectator sport. God expects you to get in the game.

"Let us run with perseverance the race marked out for us."
Hebrews 12:1 NIV

PRAYER LIST	TO DO LIST
1. _____	1. _____
2. _____	2. _____
3. _____	3. _____
4. _____	4. _____
5. _____	5. _____
6. _____	6. _____
7. _____	7. _____

Prayer journal notes:

Psalms 126-128; I Corinthians 10:19-33

_____

_____

_____

_____

_____

_____

_____

_____

_____

_____

_____

DAY 242

God only disciplines those in the family.

> *"Endure hardship as discipline; God is treating you as*
> *sons. For what son is not disciplined by his father?"*
> Hebrews 12:7 NIV

PRAYER LIST	TO DO LIST
1. _____	1. _____
2. _____	2. _____
3. _____	3. _____
4. _____	4. _____
5. _____	5. _____
6. _____	6. _____
7. _____	7. _____

Prayer journal notes:

Psalms 129-131; I Corinthians 11:1-16

_____

_____

_____

_____

_____

_____

_____

_____

_____

_____

DAY 243

Standing on Christ the solid Rock is safe and secure, but that doesn't mean we won't sometimes tremble. But one thing we can count on, Christ the solid Rock will never tremble under us.

"He alone is my rock and my salvation; He is my fortress, I will never be shaken."

Psalm 62:2 NIV

PRAYER LIST	TO DO LIST
1. _____	1. _____
2. _____	2. _____
3. _____	3. _____
4. _____	4. _____
5. _____	5. _____
6. _____	6. _____
7. _____	7. _____

Prayer journal notes:

Psalms 132-143; I Corinthians 11:17-34

_____

_____

_____

_____

_____

_____

_____

_____

DAY 244

Oh be careful little mouth what you say.
There is always someone listening.

> *"Do not let any unwholesome talk come out of your mouths, but only what is helpful for building others up according to their needs."*
>
> *Ephesians 4:29 NIV*

PRAYER LIST	TO DO LIST
1. _____	1. _____
2. _____	2. _____
3. _____	3. _____
4. _____	4. _____
5. _____	5. _____
6. _____	6. _____
7. _____	7. _____

Prayer journal notes:

Psalms 135-136; I Corinthians 12

_____

_____

_____

_____

_____

_____

_____

_____

DAY 245

Everyone who enters this world is a person of dignity. The custodian is no different than the CEO.

> *"So God created man in His own image, in the image of God He created them; male and female He created them."*
>
> Genesis 1:27 NIV

PRAYER LIST	TO DO LIST
1. _____	1. _____
2. _____	2. _____
3. _____	3. _____
4. _____	4. _____
5. _____	5. _____
6. _____	6. _____
7. _____	7. _____

Prayer journal notes:

Psalms 137-139; I Corinthians 13

_____

_____

_____

_____

_____

_____

_____

DAY 246

∽⌒◡

It's not necessarily how fast you start, but how well you finish.

"I have fought the good fight, I have finished the race, I have kept the faith."

2 Timothy 4:7 NIV

PRAYER LIST	TO DO LIST
1. _____	1. _____
2. _____	2. _____
3. _____	3. _____
4. _____	4. _____
5. _____	5. _____
6. _____	6. _____
7. _____	7. _____

Prayer journal notes:

Psalms 140-142; I Corinthians 14:1-20

_____

_____

_____

_____

_____

_____

_____

_____

_____

_____

DAY 247

Those who are tardy may miss the party. Delayed obedience is disobedience. Don't delay when God opens a window of opportunity.

"...be prepared in season and out of season."
2 Timothy 4:2 NIV

PRAYER LIST	TO DO LIST
1. _____	1. _____
2. _____	2. _____
3. _____	3. _____
4. _____	4. _____
5. _____	5. _____
6. _____	6. _____
7. _____	7. _____

Prayer journal notes:

Psalms 143-145; I Corinthians 14:21-40

_____
_____
_____
_____
_____
_____
_____
_____
_____

DAY 248

The quieter you become, the more you can hear. The more you can hear, the more you can learn. You can't learn anything new when your mouth is running.

"Let the wise listen and add to their learning."

Proverbs 1:5 NIV

PRAYER LIST	TO DO LIST
1. _____	1. _____
2. _____	2. _____
3. _____	3. _____
4. _____	4. _____
5. _____	5. _____
6. _____	6. _____
7. _____	7. _____

 Prayer journal notes:

Psalms 146-147; I Corinthians 15:1-28

_____

_____

_____

_____

_____

_____

_____

_____

_____

DAY 249

The world offers many temporary fixes. But there is a reason why the things of this world don't satisfy.

> *"For you are not of the world any more than I am of the world."*
>
> *John 14:17 NIV*

PRAYER LIST	TO DO LIST
1. _____	1. _____
2. _____	2. _____
3. _____	3. _____
4. _____	4. _____
5. _____	5. _____
6. _____	6. _____
7. _____	7. _____

Prayer journal notes:

Psalms 148-150; I Corinthians 15:29-58

_____

_____

_____

_____

_____

_____

_____

_____

_____

DAY 250

We serve God by serving others. We love God by loving others. We each have a purpose today. Be sure and fulfill it.

"Whatever you do for the least of these brothers of mine, you did for Me."

Matthew 28:40 NIV

PRAYER LIST	TO DO LIST
1. _____	1. _____
2. _____	2. _____
3. _____	3. _____
4. _____	4. _____
5. _____	5. _____
6. _____	6. _____
7. _____	7. _____

Prayer journal notes:

Proverbs 1-2; I Corinthians 16

_____

_____

_____

_____

_____

_____

_____

_____

DAY 251

Strive for God to be glorified in everything you do.

"So whether you eat or drink or whatever you do, do it all for the glory of God."

1 Corinthians 10:31 NIV

PRAYER LIST	TO DO LIST
1. _____	1. _____
2. _____	2. _____
3. _____	3. _____
4. _____	4. _____
5. _____	5. _____
6. _____	6. _____
7. _____	7. _____

Prayer journal notes:

Proverbs 3-5; II Corinthians 1

_____
_____
_____
_____
_____
_____
_____
_____
_____
_____
_____

DAY 252

When we truly care about one another, we will care for one another.

> *"I hope to visit you while passing through and to have you assist me on my journey there, after I have enjoyed your company for a while."*
>
> *Romans 15:24 NIV*

PRAYER LIST	TO DO LIST
1. _____	1. _____
2. _____	2. _____
3. _____	3. _____
4. _____	4. _____
5. _____	5. _____
6. _____	6. _____
7. _____	7. _____

Prayer journal notes:

Proverbs 6-7; II Corinthians 2

_____

_____

_____

_____

_____

_____

_____

_____

DAY 253

There is a void in your soul that will go unfilled until you are at peace with God and have the peace of God, Who created you.

"And the peace of God, which surpasses all understanding, will guard your hearts and minds through Christ Jesus."
Philippians 4:7 NKJV

PRAYER LIST	TO DO LIST
1. _____	1. _____
2. _____	2. _____
3. _____	3. _____
4. _____	4. _____
5. _____	5. _____
6. _____	6. _____
7. _____	7. _____

Prayer journal notes:

Proverbs 8-9; II Corinthians 3

_____
_____
_____
_____
_____
_____
_____
_____

DAY 254

God has a history of taking something that is broken and confused and making something beautiful and useful out of it.

"We are the clay, You are the potter; we are all the work of Your hand."

Isaiah 64:8 NIV

PRAYER LIST	TO DO LIST
1. _____	1. _____
2. _____	2. _____
3. _____	3. _____
4. _____	4. _____
5. _____	5. _____
6. _____	6. _____
7. _____	7. _____

Prayer journal notes:

Proverbs 10-12; II Corinthians 4

_____

_____

_____

_____

_____

_____

_____

_____

DAY 255

If we are not in awe of God, then we don't think enough of Him and think too much of ourselves.

"For this is what the high and lofty One says...I live in a high and holy place, but also with him who is contrite and lowly in spirit."

Isaiah 57:15 NIV

PRAYER LIST	TO DO LIST
1. _____	1. _____
2. _____	2. _____
3. _____	3. _____
4. _____	4. _____
5. _____	5. _____
6. _____	6. _____
7. _____	7. _____

Prayer journal notes:

Proverbs 13-15; II Corinthians 5

_____

_____

_____

_____

_____

_____

_____

_____

DAY 256

When something sounds too good to be true, it probably is.
Unless it is a God-thing.

> *"For the wages of sin is death, but the gift of God is
> eternal life in Christ Jesus our Lord."*
>
> Romans 6:23 NIV

PRAYER LIST	TO DO LIST
1. _____	1. _____
2. _____	2. _____
3. _____	3. _____
4. _____	4. _____
5. _____	5. _____
6. _____	6. _____
7. _____	7. _____

Prayer journal notes:

Proverbs 16-18; II Corinthians 6

_____

_____

_____

_____

_____

_____

_____

_____

_____

_____

DAY 257

Think of the person you love the most, and how much you love them. Then know that God loves you even more than that.

"May you experience the love of Christ, though it is too great to understand fully."

Ephesians 3:19 NLT

PRAYER LIST	TO DO LIST
1. _____	1. _____
2. _____	2. _____
3. _____	3. _____
4. _____	4. _____
5. _____	5. _____
6. _____	6. _____
7. _____	7. _____

Prayer journal notes:

Proverbs 19-21; II Corinthians 7

_____
_____
_____
_____
_____
_____
_____
_____

DAY 258

God may be invisible, but He is in touch and in control. He is large and in charge.

"No one will be able to stand up against you...I will be with you; I will never leave you nor forsake you."

Joshua 1:5 NIV

PRAYER LIST	TO DO LIST
1. _____	1. _____
2. _____	2. _____
3. _____	3. _____
4. _____	4. _____
5. _____	5. _____
6. _____	6. _____
7. _____	7. _____

Prayer journal notes:

Proverbs 22-24; II Corinthians 8

_____

_____

_____

_____

_____

_____

_____

_____

_____

DAY 259

Don't get hung up on a timeline. One thing you can count on, God will finish what He starts in His timing.

> *"Being confident of this, that He who began a good work in you will carry it on to completion until the day of Christ Jesus."*
>
> Philippians 1:6 NIV

PRAYER LIST	TO DO LIST
1. _____	1. _____
2. _____	2. _____
3. _____	3. _____
4. _____	4. _____
5. _____	5. _____
6. _____	6. _____
7. _____	7. _____

Prayer journal notes:

Proverbs 25-26; II Corinthians 9

_____
_____
_____
_____
_____
_____
_____
_____

DAY 260

Christianity becomes authentic for you when living for Christ becomes as natural as putting on your clothes.

"Clothe yourselves with the Lord Jesus Christ."
Romans 13:14 NIV

PRAYER LIST	TO DO LIST
1. _____	1. _____
2. _____	2. _____
3. _____	3. _____
4. _____	4. _____
5. _____	5. _____
6. _____	6. _____
7. _____	7. _____

Prayer journal notes:

Proverbs 27-29; II Corinthians 10

_____
_____
_____
_____
_____
_____
_____
_____
_____
_____
_____

DAY 261

Helping someone behind the scenes or going the extra mile may seem to go unnoticed, but it does not.

"The eyes of the Lord are everywhere, keeping watch on the wicked and the good."

Proverbs 15:3 NIV

PRAYER LIST	TO DO LIST
1. _____	1. _____
2. _____	2. _____
3. _____	3. _____
4. _____	4. _____
5. _____	5. _____
6. _____	6. _____
7. _____	7. _____

Prayer journal notes:

Proverbs 30-31; II Corinthians 11:1-15

_____

_____

_____

_____

_____

_____

_____

_____

_____

DAY 262

There is no occasion when love is inappropriate.

"Above all, love each other deeply, because love covers a multitude of sins."

1 Peter 4:8 NIV

PRAYER LIST	TO DO LIST
1. _____	1. _____
2. _____	2. _____
3. _____	3. _____
4. _____	4. _____
5. _____	5. _____
6. _____	6. _____
7. _____	7. _____

Prayer journal notes:

Ecclesiastes 1-3; II Corinthians 11:16-33

_____

_____

_____

_____

_____

_____

_____

_____

_____

_____

_____

DAY 263

〜๑

We should give grace as freely as God does to us. Our personal space should be a place of grace.

"Let your conversation always be full of grace."
Colossians 4:6 NIV

PRAYER LIST	TO DO LIST
1. _____	1. _____
2. _____	2. _____
3. _____	3. _____
4. _____	4. _____
5. _____	5. _____
6. _____	6. _____
7. _____	7. _____

Prayer journal notes:

Ecclesiastes 4-6; II Corinthians 12

_____
_____
_____
_____
_____
_____
_____
_____
_____
_____
_____

DAY 264

~⌒~

When we give our life to Christ, He does more than just make us better, He makes us new.

"And to put on the new self, created to be like God in true righteousness and holiness."

Ephesians 4:24 NIV

PRAYER LIST	TO DO LIST
1. _____	1. _____
2. _____	2. _____
3. _____	3. _____
4. _____	4. _____
5. _____	5. _____
6. _____	6. _____
7. _____	7. _____

Prayer journal notes:

Ecclesiastes 7-9; II Corinthians 13

_____

_____

_____

_____

_____

_____

_____

_____

_____

DAY 265

The search for the kingdom of God begins from within you.

"The kingdom of God does not come with your careful observation, nor will people say, 'Here it is,' or 'There it is,' because the kingdom of God is within you."

Luke 17:20-21 NIV

PRAYER LIST	TO DO LIST
1. _____	1. _____
2. _____	2. _____
3. _____	3. _____
4. _____	4. _____
5. _____	5. _____
6. _____	6. _____
7. _____	7. _____

Prayer journal notes:

Ecclesiastes 10-12; Galatians 1

_____

_____

_____

_____

_____

_____

_____

_____

_____

DAY 266

You cannot rule out something that doesn't make sense. If you want to see God laugh, tell Him something is impossible.

"What is impossible with men is possible with God."
Luke 18:27 NIV

PRAYER LIST	TO DO LIST
1. _____	1. _____
2. _____	2. _____
3. _____	3. _____
4. _____	4. _____
5. _____	5. _____
6. _____	6. _____
7. _____	7. _____

Prayer journal notes:

Song of Songs 1-3; Galatians 2

_____

_____

_____

_____

_____

_____

_____

_____

_____

_____

_____

DAY 267

Spiritual growth requires effort on your part. It will not happen on its own. It's like being on a hill of ice. You are either climbing higher, or sliding lower. There is no sitting still.

"Make every effort to be found spotless, blameless, and at peace with Him."

2 Peter 3:14 NIV

PRAYER LIST	TO DO LIST
1. _____	1. _____
2. _____	2. _____
3. _____	3. _____
4. _____	4. _____
5. _____	5. _____
6. _____	6. _____
7. _____	7. _____

Prayer journal notes:

Song of Songs 4-5; Galatians 3

_____
_____
_____
_____
_____
_____
_____
_____

DAY 268

Sometimes, like medicine, what's best for you doesn't taste very good at the time. God answers prayers based on what's best for you in the long term.

> *"Do not fear, little flock, for it is your Father's good pleasure to give you the kingdom."*
>
> Luke 12:32 NKJV

PRAYER LIST	TO DO LIST
1. _____	1. _____
2. _____	2. _____
3. _____	3. _____
4. _____	4. _____
5. _____	5. _____
6. _____	6. _____
7. _____	7. _____

Prayer journal notes:

Song of Songs 6-8; Galatians 4

_____

_____

_____

_____

_____

_____

_____

_____

DAY 269

Don't sell yourself short, when the all-powerful third member of the Trinity; the Holy Spirit, with limitless capabilities lives within you.

> *"Do you not know that you are the temple of God, and that the Spirit of God dwells in you?"*
>
> *1 Corinthians 3:16 NIV*

PRAYER LIST	TO DO LIST
1. _____	1. _____
2. _____	2. _____
3. _____	3. _____
4. _____	4. _____
5. _____	5. _____
6. _____	6. _____
7. _____	7. _____

Prayer journal notes:

Isaiah 1-2; Galatians 5

_____
_____
_____
_____
_____
_____
_____
_____

DAY 270

Does a police escort make you feel secure? You have better security than that today.

> *"For He will command His angels concerning you to guard you in all your ways."*
>
> *Psalm 91:11 NIV*

PRAYER LIST	TO DO LIST
1. _____	1. _____
2. _____	2. _____
3. _____	3. _____
4. _____	4. _____
5. _____	5. _____
6. _____	6. _____
7. _____	7. _____

Prayer journal notes:

Isaiah 3-4; Galatians 6

_____

_____

_____

_____

_____

_____

_____

_____

_____

DAY 271

The longer you have and are a friend, the more valuable your friendship becomes. Spend some time with a good friend today.

"Do not forsake your friends…"

Proverbs 27:10 NIV

PRAYER LIST	TO DO LIST
1. _____	1. _____
2. _____	2. _____
3. _____	3. _____
4. _____	4. _____
5. _____	5. _____
6. _____	6. _____
7. _____	7. _____

Prayer journal notes:

Isaiah 5-6; Ephesians 1

_____

_____

_____

_____

_____

_____

_____

_____

_____

DAY 272

When you keep God first in the little things, they amazingly grow into big things.

"Well done, good and faithful servant! You have been faithful with a few things; I will put you in charge of many things. Come and share in your Master's happiness."
Matthew 25:21 NIV

PRAYER LIST	TO DO LIST
1. _____	1. _____
2. _____	2. _____
3. _____	3. _____
4. _____	4. _____
5. _____	5. _____
6. _____	6. _____
7. _____	7. _____

Prayer journal notes:

Isaiah 7-8; Ephesians 2

_____

_____

_____

_____

_____

_____

_____

_____

DAY 273

Your biggest blessing comes when you are a blessing to someone else, expecting nothing in return.

> *"I will send down showers...there will be showers of blessing."*
>
> Ezekiel 34:26 NIV

PRAYER LIST	TO DO LIST
1. _____	1. _____
2. _____	2. _____
3. _____	3. _____
4. _____	4. _____
5. _____	5. _____
6. _____	6. _____
7. _____	7. _____

Prayer journal notes:

Isaiah 9-10; Ephesians 3

_____

_____

_____

_____

_____

_____

_____

_____

DAY 274

In fulfilling your purpose on earth, there is only one person you have to please. If you are pleasing God, everything else will fall into place.

"Our purpose is to please God, not people."
1 Thessalonians 2:4 NLT

PRAYER LIST	TO DO LIST
1. _____	1. _____
2. _____	2. _____
3. _____	3. _____
4. _____	4. _____
5. _____	5. _____
6. _____	6. _____
7. _____	7. _____

Prayer journal notes:

Isaiah 11-13; Ephesians 4

_____

_____

_____

_____

_____

_____

_____

_____

_____

_____

DAY 275

Be a tree - with roots deeply entrenched in your faith in God.

"He is like a tree planted by streams of water, which yields its fruit in season and whose leaf does not wither. Whatever he does prospers."

Psalm 1:3 NIV

PRAYER LIST	TO DO LIST
1. _____	1. _____
2. _____	2. _____
3. _____	3. _____
4. _____	4. _____
5. _____	5. _____
6. _____	6. _____
7. _____	7. _____

Prayer journal notes:

Isaiah 14-16; Ephesians 5:1-16

_____

_____

_____

_____

_____

_____

_____

_____

DAY 276

Our God is not dull, boring, or mediocre, and He doesn't expect His children to be.
Have an exciting day!

"For the Lord your God who is among you, is a great and awesome God."

Deuteronomy 7:21NIV

PRAYER LIST	TO DO LIST
1. _____	1. _____
2. _____	2. _____
3. _____	3. _____
4. _____	4. _____
5. _____	5. _____
6. _____	6. _____
7. _____	7. _____

Prayer journal notes:

Isaiah 17-19; Ephesians 5:17-33

_____

_____

_____

_____

_____

_____

_____

_____

DAY 277

You will be more efficient and effective when you enjoy and have fun doing what you are doing. You attitude determines your altitude.

"For the joy of the Lord is your strength."

Nehemiah 8:10 NIV

PRAYER LIST	TO DO LIST
1. _____	1. _____
2. _____	2. _____
3. _____	3. _____
4. _____	4. _____
5. _____	5. _____
6. _____	6. _____
7. _____	7. _____

Prayer journal notes:

Isaiah 20-22; Ephesians 6

_____

_____

_____

_____

_____

_____

_____

_____

_____

DAY 278

Don't work so much that you aren't productive. You are not at your best unless you get some rest.

"In vain you rise up early and stay up late, toiling for food to eat -- for He grants sleep to those He loves."
Psalm 127:2 NIV

PRAYER LIST	TO DO LIST
1. _____	1. _____
2. _____	2. _____
3. _____	3. _____
4. _____	4. _____
5. _____	5. _____
6. _____	6. _____
7. _____	7. _____

Prayer journal notes:

Isaiah 23-25; Philippians 1

_____

_____

_____

_____

_____

_____

_____

_____

DAY 279

⌒◯

Someone do you wrong? Stab you in the back? Revenge is not for you to take. Let go and let God have it. He can handle it much better than you.

"Do not take revenge, my friends, but leave room for God's wrath, for it is written: 'It is mine to avenge; I will repay,' says the Lord."

Luke 18:27 NIV

PRAYER LIST	TO DO LIST
1. _____	1. _____
2. _____	2. _____
3. _____	3. _____
4. _____	4. _____
5. _____	5. _____
6. _____	6. _____
7. _____	7. _____

Prayer journal notes:

Isaiah 26-27; Philippians 2

_____

_____

_____

_____

_____

_____

_____

_____

DAY 280

Your attitude is noticed by everyone around you. Be humbly grateful, not grumbly hateful.

"Offer hospitality to one another without grumbling."
1 Peter 4:9 NIV

PRAYER LIST	TO DO LIST
1. _____	1. _____
2. _____	2. _____
3. _____	3. _____
4. _____	4. _____
5. _____	5. _____
6. _____	6. _____
7. _____	7. _____

Prayer journal notes:

Isaiah 28-29; Philippians 3

_____

_____

_____

_____

_____

_____

_____

_____

_____

_____

DAY 281

If you stop and count your blessings, you realize you have a lot to be thankful for. Everything you are, everything you have; give thanks to God.

"The Lord has done great things for us and we are filled with joy."

Psalm 126:3 NIV

PRAYER LIST	TO DO LIST
1. _____	1. _____
2. _____	2. _____
3. _____	3. _____
4. _____	4. _____
5. _____	5. _____
6. _____	6. _____
7. _____	7. _____

Prayer journal notes:

Isaiah 30-31; Philippians 4

_____
_____
_____
_____
_____
_____
_____
_____

DAY 282

You are too blessed to be stressed, too favored to waiver. You are royalty, an heir of the King.

> *"Now if we are children, then we are heirs — heirs of God and co-heirs with Christ."*
>
> Romans 8:17 NIV

PRAYER LIST	TO DO LIST
1. _____	1. _____
2. _____	2. _____
3. _____	3. _____
4. _____	4. _____
5. _____	5. _____
6. _____	6. _____
7. _____	7. _____

Prayer journal notes:

Isaiah 32-33; Colossians 1

_____

_____

_____

_____

_____

_____

_____

_____

_____

DAY 283

It's always too early to give up. Things of great value that you will be proud of are always worth the struggle.

"Perseverance must finish its work so that you may be mature and complete, not lacking anything."

James 1:4 NIV

PRAYER LIST	TO DO LIST
1. _____	1. _____
2. _____	2. _____
3. _____	3. _____
4. _____	4. _____
5. _____	5. _____
6. _____	6. _____
7. _____	7. _____

Prayer journal notes:

Isaiah 34-36; Colossians 2

_____

_____

_____

_____

_____

_____

_____

_____

_____

DAY 284

There's nothing you can do to blow God's plans for your life. Don't be discouraged if it's not the route you originally wanted to take. Follow God's lead and enjoy the scenery.

> *"I know that You can do all things; no plan of Yours can be thwarted."*
>
> Job 42:2 NIV

PRAYER LIST	TO DO LIST
1. _____	1. _____
2. _____	2. _____
3. _____	3. _____
4. _____	4. _____
5. _____	5. _____
6. _____	6. _____
7. _____	7. _____

Prayer journal notes:

Isaiah 37-38; Colossians 3

_____

_____

_____

_____

_____

_____

_____

_____

DAY 285

God will never put you in the wrong place to serve Him. There is no place God won't use you.

"Serve one another in love."

Galatians 5:13 NIV

PRAYER LIST	TO DO LIST
1. _____	1. _____
2. _____	2. _____
3. _____	3. _____
4. _____	4. _____
5. _____	5. _____
6. _____	6. _____
7. _____	7. _____

Prayer journal notes:

Isaiah 39-40; Colossians 4

_____

_____

_____

_____

_____

_____

_____

_____

_____

_____

DAY 286

You become whatever you are committed to.
You find time for your top priorities.

*"Do not conform any longer to the pattern of this world,
but be transformed…"*

Romans 12:2 NIV

PRAYER LIST	TO DO LIST
1. _____	1. _____
2. _____	2. _____
3. _____	3. _____
4. _____	4. _____
5. _____	5. _____
6. _____	6. _____
7. _____	7. _____

Prayer journal notes:

Isaiah 41-42; I Thessalonians 1

_____

_____

_____

_____

_____

_____

_____

_____

_____

DAY 287

Pardon the interruption, but when God interrupts your life, it's always in your best interest.

"The plans of the Lord stand firm forever."

Psalm 33:11 NIV

PRAYER LIST	TO DO LIST
1. _____	1. _____
2. _____	2. _____
3. _____	3. _____
4. _____	4. _____
5. _____	5. _____
6. _____	6. _____
7. _____	7. _____

Prayer journal notes:

Isaiah 43-44; I Thessalonians 2

_____

_____

_____

_____

_____

_____

_____

_____

_____

_____

DAY 288

Even great kings know the importance of prayer during stressful times.

"David was greatly distressed for the people spoke of stoning him…but David strengthened himself in the Lord his God."

1 Samuel 30:6 NKJV

PRAYER LIST	TO DO LIST
1. _____	1. _____
2. _____	2. _____
3. _____	3. _____
4. _____	4. _____
5. _____	5. _____
6. _____	6. _____
7. _____	7. _____

Prayer journal notes:

Isaiah 45-46; I Thessalonians 3

_____

_____

_____

_____

_____

_____

_____

_____

DAY 289

Whatever storm life throws at you today, you have hope to cope. Dig in and hold on tight. The anchor holds in spite of the storm.

"We have God's promised hope as an anchor, firm and secure."

Hebrews 6:19 NIV

PRAYER LIST	TO DO LIST
1. _____	1. _____
2. _____	2. _____
3. _____	3. _____
4. _____	4. _____
5. _____	5. _____
6. _____	6. _____
7. _____	7. _____

Prayer journal notes:

Isaiah 47-49; I Thessalonians 4

_____

_____

_____

_____

_____

_____

_____

DAY 290

You get a maximum return on your investment when you invest in those who are making a kingdom difference.

"I tell you, use worldly wealth to gain friends for yourselves, so that when it is gone, you will be welcomed into eternal dwellings."

Luke 16:9 NIV

PRAYER LIST	TO DO LIST
1. _____	1. _____
2. _____	2. _____
3. _____	3. _____
4. _____	4. _____
5. _____	5. _____
6. _____	6. _____
7. _____	7. _____

Prayer journal notes:

Isaiah 50-52; I Thessalonians 5

_____

_____

_____

_____

_____

_____

_____

_____

DAY 291

Don't go and create a storm and then get mad when you are struck by lightning.

> *"Blessed are the peacemakers, for they will be called sons of God."*
>
> Matthew 5:9 NIV

PRAYER LIST	TO DO LIST
1. _____	1. _____
2. _____	2. _____
3. _____	3. _____
4. _____	4. _____
5. _____	5. _____
6. _____	6. _____
7. _____	7. _____

Prayer journal notes:

Isaiah 53-55; II Thessalonians 1

_____
_____
_____
_____
_____
_____
_____
_____
_____

DAY 292

Peace is not the absence of trouble. It is the presence of God. If you are not running head on with Satan, then you are probably running in the same direction.

"Therefore since we have been justified through faith, we have peace with God through our Lord Jesus Christ."

Romans 5:1 NIV

PRAYER LIST	TO DO LIST
1. _____	1. _____
2. _____	2. _____
3. _____	3. _____
4. _____	4. _____
5. _____	5. _____
6. _____	6. _____
7. _____	7. _____

Prayer journal notes:

Isaiah 56-58; II Thessalonians 2

_____

_____

_____

_____

_____

_____

_____

_____

DAY 293

Having joy in the Lord is more contagious than a virus. May others catch it from you today!

> *"So that through my being with you again your joy in Christ Jesus will overflow on account of me."*
> Philippians 1:26 NIV

PRAYER LIST	TO DO LIST
1. _____	1. _____
2. _____	2. _____
3. _____	3. _____
4. _____	4. _____
5. _____	5. _____
6. _____	6. _____
7. _____	7. _____

Prayer journal notes:

Isaiah 59-61; II Thessalonians 3

_____

_____

_____

_____

_____

_____

_____

_____

_____

DAY 294

∽

Life is short, death is sure. Sin the cause, Christ the cure.

"For the wages of sin is death, but the gift of God is eternal life in Christ Jesus our Lord."

Romans 6:23 NIV

PRAYER LIST	TO DO LIST
1. _____	1. _____
2. _____	2. _____
3. _____	3. _____
4. _____	4. _____
5. _____	5. _____
6. _____	6. _____
7. _____	7. _____

Prayer journal notes:

Isaiah 62-64; I Timothy 1

_____

_____

_____

_____

_____

_____

_____

_____

_____

_____

DAY 295

Today's opportunities always take precedence over tomorrow's possibilities. We have no promise of tomorrow.

"Why, you do not even know what will happen tomorrow."
James 4:14 NIV

PRAYER LIST	TO DO LIST
1. _____	1. _____
2. _____	2. _____
3. _____	3. _____
4. _____	4. _____
5. _____	5. _____
6. _____	6. _____
7. _____	7. _____

Prayer journal notes:

Isaiah 65-66; I Timothy 2

_____

_____

_____

_____

_____

_____

_____

_____

_____

_____

DAY 296

There are times when the best thing to do is to stop, breathe, and do nothing. There are some battles that you just need to stay out of.

"Be still and know that I am God."

Psalm 46:10 NIV

PRAYER LIST	TO DO LIST
1. _____	1. _____
2. _____	2. _____
3. _____	3. _____
4. _____	4. _____
5. _____	5. _____
6. _____	6. _____
7. _____	7. _____

Prayer journal notes:

Jeremiah 1-2; I Timothy 3

_____

_____

_____

_____

_____

_____

_____

_____

_____

_____

DAY 297

Never be bothered by other people's criticism. You can't make yourself sick trying to make someone else well.

> *"See to it that no one takes you captive through hollow and deceptive philosophy, which depends on human tradition and the basic principles of this world rather than on Christ."*
>
> *Colossians 2:8 NIV*

PRAYER LIST

1. _____
2. _____
3. _____
4. _____
5. _____
6. _____
7. _____

TO DO LIST

1. _____
2. _____
3. _____
4. _____
5. _____
6. _____
7. _____

Prayer journal notes:

Jeremiah 3-5; I Timothy 4

_____

_____

_____

_____

_____

_____

_____

_____

DAY 298

God has called us to play the game, but not to keep score. We are to be witnesses in the courtroom of life, but not the judge.

"Who are you to judge your neighbor?"

James 4:12 NIV

PRAYER LIST	TO DO LIST
1. _____	1. _____
2. _____	2. _____
3. _____	3. _____
4. _____	4. _____
5. _____	5. _____
6. _____	6. _____
7. _____	7. _____

Prayer journal notes:

Jeremiah 6-8; I Timothy 5

_____

_____

_____

_____

_____

_____

_____

_____

_____

DAY 299

The best things in life aren't things. Your true wealth is a total of everything you have that money can't buy and death can't take away. Don't be so poor, all you have is money.

> *"We live on...sorrowful, yet always rejoicing...poor, yet making many rich; having nothing, and yet possessing everything."*
>
> *2 Corinthians 6:9-10 NIV*

PRAYER LIST	TO DO LIST
1. _____	1. _____
2. _____	2. _____
3. _____	3. _____
4. _____	4. _____
5. _____	5. _____
6. _____	6. _____
7. _____	7. _____

Prayer journal notes:

Jeremiah 9-11; I Timothy 6

_____
_____
_____
_____
_____
_____
_____
_____

DAY 300

Be willing to go above and beyond. Don't just meet expectations, exceed expectations.

"We are unworthy servants, we have only done our duty."
Luke 17:10 NIV

PRAYER LIST

1. _____
2. _____
3. _____
4. _____
5. _____
6. _____
7. _____

TO DO LIST

1. _____
2. _____
3. _____
4. _____
5. _____
6. _____
7. _____

Prayer journal notes:

Jeremiah 12-14; II Timothy 1

_____

_____

_____

_____

_____

_____

_____

_____

_____

_____

DAY 301

You can always rely on God to give you the right words to say at the right time.

"The Lord said to him...'I will help you speak and teach you what to say.'"

Exodus 4:11-12 NIV

PRAYER LIST	TO DO LIST
1. _____	1. _____
2. _____	2. _____
3. _____	3. _____
4. _____	4. _____
5. _____	5. _____
6. _____	6. _____
7. _____	7. _____

Prayer journal notes:

Jeremiah 15-17; II Timothy 2

_____

_____

_____

_____

_____

_____

_____

_____

_____

DAY 302

God conceals His surprises until we follow His lead. A step of obedience in faith results in major blessings.

"And as they went, they were cleansed."

Luke 17:14 NIV

PRAYER LIST	TO DO LIST
1. _____	1. _____
2. _____	2. _____
3. _____	3. _____
4. _____	4. _____
5. _____	5. _____
6. _____	6. _____
7. _____	7. _____

Prayer journal notes:

Jeremiah 18-19; II Timothy 3

_____

_____

_____

_____

_____

_____

_____

_____

_____

_____

_____

DAY 303

There cannot be a return on an investment that is not invested.
A seed will never grow unless it is planted.

"He who sows righteousness reaps a sure reward."
Proverbs 11:18 NIV

PRAYER LIST	TO DO LIST
1. _____	1. _____
2. _____	2. _____
3. _____	3. _____
4. _____	4. _____
5. _____	5. _____
6. _____	6. _____
7. _____	7. _____

Prayer journal notes:

Jeremiah 20-21; II Timothy 4

_____
_____
_____
_____
_____
_____
_____
_____
_____
_____

DAY 304

While you were asleep all night, God was not. He was busy preparing to bless you today.

"He will never let me stumble, slip or fall. For He is always watching, never sleeping."

Psalm 121:3 TLB

PRAYER LIST	TO DO LIST
1. _____	1. _____
2. _____	2. _____
3. _____	3. _____
4. _____	4. _____
5. _____	5. _____
6. _____	6. _____
7. _____	7. _____

Prayer journal notes:

Jeremiah 22-23; Titus 1

_____

_____

_____

_____

_____

_____

_____

_____

_____

DAY 305

When you know your future is secure, you can concentrate on your present. Yesterday and tomorrow can be removed from your calendar of concerns.

"There is surely a future hope for you..."

Proverbs 23:18 NIV

PRAYER LIST	TO DO LIST
1. _____	1. _____
2. _____	2. _____
3. _____	3. _____
4. _____	4. _____
5. _____	5. _____
6. _____	6. _____
7. _____	7. _____

Prayer journal notes:

Jeremiah 24-26; Titus 2

_____

_____

_____

_____

_____

_____

_____

_____

DAY 306

There are those who are never satisfied. And then there are those who trust Jesus.

> *"For He satisfies the thirsty and fills the hungry with good things."*
>
> Psalm 107:9 NIV

PRAYER LIST	TO DO LIST
1. _____	1. _____
2. _____	2. _____
3. _____	3. _____
4. _____	4. _____
5. _____	5. _____
6. _____	6. _____
7. _____	7. _____

Prayer journal notes:

Jeremiah 27-29; Titus 3

_____

_____

_____

_____

_____

_____

_____

_____

_____

DAY 307

Before you ask God to change someone else to improve a relationship, be sure you are first willing to change yourself.

"Create in me a pure heart, O God, and renew a steadfast spirit within me."

Psalm 51:10 NIV

PRAYER LIST	TO DO LIST
1. _____	1. _____
2. _____	2. _____
3. _____	3. _____
4. _____	4. _____
5. _____	5. _____
6. _____	6. _____
7. _____	7. _____

Prayer journal notes:

Jeremiah 30-31; Philemon

_____

_____

_____

_____

_____

_____

_____

_____

DAY 308

You can determine your priorities by your checkbook and your calendar; what you spend the most time and money on.

"What good is it for a man to gain the whole world, yet forfeit his soul?"

Mark 8:36 NIV

PRAYER LIST	TO DO LIST
1. _____	1. _____
2. _____	2. _____
3. _____	3. _____
4. _____	4. _____
5. _____	5. _____
6. _____	6. _____
7. _____	7. _____

Prayer journal notes:

Jeremiah 32-33; Hebrews 1

_____

_____

_____

_____

_____

_____

_____

_____

_____

DAY 309

Some of the ugliest people are beautiful on the outside. Beauty goes much further than skin deep; it goes heart deep.

"The Lord does not look at the things man looks at. Man looks at the outward appearance, but the Lord looks at the heart."

1 Samuel 16:7 NIV

PRAYER LIST	TO DO LIST
1. _____	1. _____
2. _____	2. _____
3. _____	3. _____
4. _____	4. _____
5. _____	5. _____
6. _____	6. _____
7. _____	7. _____

Prayer journal notes:

Jeremiah 34-36; Hebrews 2

_____
_____
_____
_____
_____
_____
_____
_____

DAY 310

The experience of life's valleys help us to better appreciate the experience of life's mountaintops.

"...why am I depriving myself of enjoyment?"
Ecclesiastes 4:8 NIV

PRAYER LIST	TO DO LIST
1. _____	1. _____
2. _____	2. _____
3. _____	3. _____
4. _____	4. _____
5. _____	5. _____
6. _____	6. _____
7. _____	7. _____

Prayer journal notes:

Jeremiah 37-39; Hebrews 3

_____

_____

_____

_____

_____

_____

_____

_____

_____

_____

_____

DAY 311

For God so loved the world (His love is plentiful), that He gave His only begotten Son (His love is priceless), that whosoever believes in Him (His love is personal), will not perish (His love is protective), but have everlasting life (His love is permanent).

John 3:16 KJV

PRAYER LIST	TO DO LIST
1. _____	1. _____
2. _____	2. _____
3. _____	3. _____
4. _____	4. _____
5. _____	5. _____
6. _____	6. _____
7. _____	7. _____

Prayer journal notes:

Jeremiah 40-42; Hebrews 4

_____

_____

_____

_____

_____

_____

_____

_____

_____

DAY 312

There is a message for us in every storm. The wind may blow us around, but those with deep roots will make it through.

"That you, being rooted and established in love, may have power...to grasp how wide and long and high and deep is the love of Christ."

1 Corinthians 3:17-18 NIV

PRAYER LIST	TO DO LIST
1. _____	1. _____
2. _____	2. _____
3. _____	3. _____
4. _____	4. _____
5. _____	5. _____
6. _____	6. _____
7. _____	7. _____

Prayer journal notes:

Jeremiah 43-45; Hebrews 5

_____

_____

_____

_____

_____

_____

_____

_____

DAY 313

Never stop praying. Persevering prayer and believing that God will answer go hand in hand.

"And will not God bring about justice for His chosen ones, who cry out to Him day and night?"

Luke 18:7 NIV

PRAYER LIST	TO DO LIST
1. _____	1. _____
2. _____	2. _____
3. _____	3. _____
4. _____	4. _____
5. _____	5. _____
6. _____	6. _____
7. _____	7. _____

Prayer journal notes:

Jeremiah 46-47; Hebrews 6

_____

_____

_____

_____

_____

_____

_____

_____

_____

DAY 314

⊂~⊃

It's not as much about who you are or where you are from, as it is whose you are and where you are going.

"Those who are led by the Spirit of God are sons of God."
Romans 8:14 NIV

PRAYER LIST	TO DO LIST
1. _____	1. _____
2. _____	2. _____
3. _____	3. _____
4. _____	4. _____
5. _____	5. _____
6. _____	6. _____
7. _____	7. _____

Prayer journal notes:

Jeremiah 48-49; Hebrews 7

_____

_____

_____

_____

_____

_____

_____

_____

_____

_____

DAY 315

The best time to praise God is always right now. Pray and praise without ceasing.

> *"I will bless the Lord at all times; His praise shall continually be in my mouth."*
>
> Psalm 34:1 NKJV

PRAYER LIST	TO DO LIST
1. _____	1. _____
2. _____	2. _____
3. _____	3. _____
4. _____	4. _____
5. _____	5. _____
6. _____	6. _____
7. _____	7. _____

Prayer journal notes:

Jeremiah 50; Hebrews 8

_____

_____

_____

_____

_____

_____

_____

_____

_____

DAY 316

You don't realize how much your mother taught you until you get older and find yourself doing and saying things she did and said.

"...and do not forsake your mother's teaching."

Proverbs 1:8 NIV

PRAYER LIST	TO DO LIST
1. _____	1. _____
2. _____	2. _____
3. _____	3. _____
4. _____	4. _____
5. _____	5. _____
6. _____	6. _____
7. _____	7. _____

Prayer journal notes:

Jeremiah 51-52; Hebrews 9

_____

_____

_____

_____

_____

_____

_____

_____

_____

DAY 317

Knowing God's will for your life begins with knowing what the Bible says. God's will is never contradictory to God's Word.

"As for God, His way is perfect; the Word of the Lord is flawless."

2 Samuel 22:31 NIV

PRAYER LIST	TO DO LIST
1. _____	1. _____
2. _____	2. _____
3. _____	3. _____
4. _____	4. _____
5. _____	5. _____
6. _____	6. _____
7. _____	7. _____

Prayer journal notes:

Lamentations 1-2; Hebrews 10:1-18

_____
_____
_____
_____
_____
_____
_____
_____
_____
_____

DAY 318

You can empathize with others only when you have been in their shoes. There is no testimony if you haven't taken the test.

"After the suffering of his soul, he will see the light of life and be satisfied."

Isaiah 53:11 NIV

PRAYER LIST	TO DO LIST
1. _____	1. _____
2. _____	2. _____
3. _____	3. _____
4. _____	4. _____
5. _____	5. _____
6. _____	6. _____
7. _____	7. _____

Prayer journal notes:

Lamentations 3-5; Hebrews 10:19-39

_____
_____
_____
_____
_____
_____
_____
_____

DAY 319

Everyone needs a quiet, uninterrupted place to talk with God. A personal altar can alter a person.

"Jesus often withdrew to lonely places and prayed."
Luke 5:16 NIV

PRAYER LIST	TO DO LIST
1. _____	1. _____
2. _____	2. _____
3. _____	3. _____
4. _____	4. _____
5. _____	5. _____
6. _____	6. _____
7. _____	7. _____

Prayer journal notes:

Ezekiel 1-2; Hebrews 11:1-19

_____
_____
_____
_____
_____
_____
_____
_____
_____
_____
_____

DAY 320

God's mercy is bigger than any mistake you have ever made or will ever make.

> *"For the Lord your God is a merciful God; He will not abandon you."*
>
> Deuteronomy 4:31 NIV

PRAYER LIST	TO DO LIST
1. _____	1. _____
2. _____	2. _____
3. _____	3. _____
4. _____	4. _____
5. _____	5. _____
6. _____	6. _____
7. _____	7. _____

Prayer journal notes:

Ezekiel 3-4; Hebrews 11:20-40

_____

_____

_____

_____

_____

_____

_____

_____

_____

_____

DAY 321

We can't sit still and go with God. God is on the move. We will either run with Him or be left behind.

> *"I run in the path of Your commands, for You have set my heart free."*
>
> *Psalm 119:32 NIV*

PRAYER LIST	TO DO LIST
1. _____	1. _____
2. _____	2. _____
3. _____	3. _____
4. _____	4. _____
5. _____	5. _____
6. _____	6. _____
7. _____	7. _____

Prayer journal notes:

Ezekiel 5-7; Hebrews 12

_____

_____

_____

_____

_____

_____

_____

_____

DAY 322

You were not created to just exist. God has a purpose for your life. He has called you to a unique mission, perfectly suited for the way He has created you.

> *"For we are God's workmanship, created in Christ Jesus to do good works, which God prepared in advance for us to do."*
>
> Ephesians 2:10 NIV

PRAYER LIST	TO DO LIST
1. _____	1. _____
2. _____	2. _____
3. _____	3. _____
4. _____	4. _____
5. _____	5. _____
6. _____	6. _____
7. _____	7. _____

Prayer journal notes:

Ezekiel 8-10; Hebrews 13

_____

_____

_____

_____

_____

_____

_____

_____

DAY 323

Troubles and trials in our lives are invitations for us to get closer to God.

"The Lord is near to all who call on Him."

Psalm 145:18 NIV

PRAYER LIST	TO DO LIST
1. _____	1. _____
2. _____	2. _____
3. _____	3. _____
4. _____	4. _____
5. _____	5. _____
6. _____	6. _____
7. _____	7. _____

Prayer journal notes:

Ezekiel 11-13; James 1

_____

_____

_____

_____

_____

_____

_____

_____

_____

_____

DAY 324

Amen does not mean goodbye. After talking with God, He is willing to help you put what He said into action.

"Jesus…went off to a solitary place, where He prayed… so He traveled throughout Galilee, preaching…and driving out demons."

Mark 1:35-39 NIV

PRAYER LIST	TO DO LIST
1. _____	1. _____
2. _____	2. _____
3. _____	3. _____
4. _____	4. _____
5. _____	5. _____
6. _____	6. _____
7. _____	7. _____

Prayer journal notes:

Ezekiel 14-15; James 2

_____

_____

_____

_____

_____

_____

_____

_____

DAY 325

Instead of venting, pray. Venting gains you sympathy. Praying gains you strength.

> *"The Lord is my strength and my shield; my heart trusts in Him, and I am helped."*
>
> *Psalm 28:7 NIV*

PRAYER LIST	TO DO LIST
1. _____	1. _____
2. _____	2. _____
3. _____	3. _____
4. _____	4. _____
5. _____	5. _____
6. _____	6. _____
7. _____	7. _____

Prayer journal notes:

Ezekiel 16-17; James 3

_____

_____

_____

_____

_____

_____

_____

_____

_____

DAY 326

A bad attitude is like a flat tire. Until you change it, you will go nowhere.

> *"Your attitude should be the same as that of Christ Jesus; who…made Himself nothing, taking the very nature of a servant."*
>
> *Philippians 2:5-7 NIV*

PRAYER LIST	TO DO LIST
1. _____	1. _____
2. _____	2. _____
3. _____	3. _____
4. _____	4. _____
5. _____	5. _____
6. _____	6. _____
7. _____	7. _____

Prayer journal notes:

Ezekiel 18-19; James 4

_____

_____

_____

_____

_____

_____

_____

_____

DAY 327

God would rather see an atheist who is kind than a Christian who is hateful.

> *"We put no stumbling block in anyone's path, so that our ministry will not be discredited."*
>
> 2 Corinthians 6:3 NIV

PRAYER LIST	TO DO LIST
1. _____	1. _____
2. _____	2. _____
3. _____	3. _____
4. _____	4. _____
5. _____	5. _____
6. _____	6. _____
7. _____	7. _____

Prayer journal notes:

Ezekiel 20-21; James 5

_____

_____

_____

_____

_____

_____

_____

_____

_____

DAY 328

Hoping for change rarely brings about change. The person who is waiting for something to turn up might start with his own sleeves.

"All hard work brings a profit, but mere talk leads only to poverty."

Proverbs 14:23 NIV

PRAYER LIST	TO DO LIST
1. _____	1. _____
2. _____	2. _____
3. _____	3. _____
4. _____	4. _____
5. _____	5. _____
6. _____	6. _____
7. _____	7. _____

Prayer journal notes:

Ezekiel 22-23; I Peter 1

_____
_____
_____
_____
_____
_____
_____
_____

DAY 329

You will never defeat your demons if you enjoy them hanging around.

"Do not be overcome by evil, but overcome evil with good."
Romans 12:21 NIV

PRAYER LIST	TO DO LIST
1. _____	1. _____
2. _____	2. _____
3. _____	3. _____
4. _____	4. _____
5. _____	5. _____
6. _____	6. _____
7. _____	7. _____

Prayer journal notes:

Ezekiel 24-26; I Peter 2

_____

_____

_____

_____

_____

_____

_____

_____

_____

_____

DAY 330

Young at heart does not mean immature at heart. God expects us to grow up.

> *"When I was a child, I talked like a child, I thought like a child, I reasoned like a child. When I became a man, I put childish ways behind me."*
>
> 1 Corinthians 13:11 NIV

PRAYER LIST	TO DO LIST
1. _____	1. _____
2. _____	2. _____
3. _____	3. _____
4. _____	4. _____
5. _____	5. _____
6. _____	6. _____
7. _____	7. _____

Prayer journal notes:

Ezekiel 27-29; I Peter 3

_____

_____

_____

_____

_____

_____

_____

_____

DAY 331

If we look deep enough into anything that is good, we find it
originated with God.

"For everything God created is good."

1 Timothy 4:4 NIV

PRAYER LIST	TO DO LIST
1. _____	1. _____
2. _____	2. _____
3. _____	3. _____
4. _____	4. _____
5. _____	5. _____
6. _____	6. _____
7. _____	7. _____

Prayer journal notes:

Ezekiel 30-32; I Peter 4

_____
_____
_____
_____
_____
_____
_____
_____
_____
_____

DAY 332

Give thanks to God with a grateful heart for all things, knowing that our every breath is dependent upon Him.

> *"Enter His gates with thanksgiving and His courts with praise; give thanks to Him and praise His name, for the Lord is good and His love endures forever."*
>
> *Psalm 100:4-5 NIV*

PRAYER LIST	TO DO LIST
1. _____	1. _____
2. _____	2. _____
3. _____	3. _____
4. _____	4. _____
5. _____	5. _____
6. _____	6. _____
7. _____	7. _____

Prayer journal notes:

Ezekiel 33-34; I Peter 5

_____

_____

_____

_____

_____

_____

_____

_____

DAY 333

If you don't teach your children to follow Jesus, the world will teach them not to. You can't spend an eternity with any of your material things, but you can your children.

> *"Train a child in the way he should go, and when he is old he will not depart from it."*
>
> Proverbs 22:6 NIV

PRAYER LIST	TO DO LIST
1. _____	1. _____
2. _____	2. _____
3. _____	3. _____
4. _____	4. _____
5. _____	5. _____
6. _____	6. _____
7. _____	7. _____

Prayer journal notes:

Ezekiel 35-36; II Peter 1

_____

_____

_____

_____

_____

_____

_____

_____

DAY 334

The gift of generosity is like a rare diamond. Few have it, but for those who do, they sparkle.

"Good will come to him who is generous."

Psalm 112:5 NIV

PRAYER LIST	TO DO LIST
1. _____	1. _____
2. _____	2. _____
3. _____	3. _____
4. _____	4. _____
5. _____	5. _____
6. _____	6. _____
7. _____	7. _____

Prayer journal notes:

Ezekiel 37-39; II Peter 2

_____

_____

_____

_____

_____

_____

_____

_____

_____

_____

DAY 335

God has lots of titles, depending upon our needs. In times of trouble, God, our Comforter; will become God, our Rescuer; and then God, our Deliverer.

"Call upon Me in the day of trouble; I will deliver you, and you will honor Me."

Psalm 50:15 NIV

PRAYER LIST	TO DO LIST
1. _____	1. _____
2. _____	2. _____
3. _____	3. _____
4. _____	4. _____
5. _____	5. _____
6. _____	6. _____
7. _____	7. _____

Prayer journal notes:

Ezekiel 40-41; II Peter 3

_____

_____

_____

_____

_____

_____

_____

_____

DAY 336

Don't underestimate your net worth. You have wealth the world cannot see and your bank account does not reflect.

"For in Him you have been enriched in every way."
1 Corinthians 1:5 NIV

PRAYER LIST	TO DO LIST
1. _____	1. _____
2. _____	2. _____
3. _____	3. _____
4. _____	4. _____
5. _____	5. _____
6. _____	6. _____
7. _____	7. _____

Prayer journal notes:

Ezekiel 42-44; I John 1

_____

_____

_____

_____

_____

_____

_____

_____

_____

_____

_____

DAY 337

You can give without loving, but you cannot love without giving.

"It is more blessed to give than to receive."

Acts 20:35 NIV

PRAYER LIST	TO DO LIST
1. _____	1. _____
2. _____	2. _____
3. _____	3. _____
4. _____	4. _____
5. _____	5. _____
6. _____	6. _____
7. _____	7. _____

Prayer journal notes:

Ezekiel 45-46; I John 2

_____

_____

_____

_____

_____

_____

_____

_____

_____

_____

DAY 338

In every desert of heartache and trouble, God will provide an oasis of comfort.

"For the Lord comforts His people"

Isaiah 49:13 NIV

PRAYER LIST	TO DO LIST
1. _____	1. _____
2. _____	2. _____
3. _____	3. _____
4. _____	4. _____
5. _____	5. _____
6. _____	6. _____
7. _____	7. _____

Prayer journal notes:

Ezekiel 47-48; I John 3

_____

_____

_____

_____

_____

_____

_____

_____

_____

_____

DAY 339

It is just as important that you do the things you know you should do as it is not to do the things you know you should not do.

"Anyone then, who knows the good he ought to do and doesn't do it, sins."

James 4:17 NIV

PRAYER LIST	TO DO LIST
1. _____	1. _____
2. _____	2. _____
3. _____	3. _____
4. _____	4. _____
5. _____	5. _____
6. _____	6. _____
7. _____	7. _____

Prayer journal notes:

Daniel 1-2; I John 4

_____

_____

_____

_____

_____

_____

_____

DAY 340

You demonstrate how smart you really are when you ask God for wisdom.

> *"If any of you lacks wisdom, he should ask God, who gives generously to all."*
>
> James 1:5 NIV

PRAYER LIST	TO DO LIST
1. _____	1. _____
2. _____	2. _____
3. _____	3. _____
4. _____	4. _____
5. _____	5. _____
6. _____	6. _____
7. _____	7. _____

Prayer journal notes:

Daniel 3-4; I John 5

_____
_____
_____
_____
_____
_____
_____
_____
_____

DAY 341

God's rules do not restrict us. They free us from all the bad things God does not want us to be hurt by.

"The Lord commanded...so we might always prosper."
Deuteronomy 6:24 NIV

PRAYER LIST	TO DO LIST
1. _____	1. _____
2. _____	2. _____
3. _____	3. _____
4. _____	4. _____
5. _____	5. _____
6. _____	6. _____
7. _____	7. _____

Prayer journal notes:

Daniel 5-7; II John

_____

_____

_____

_____

_____

_____

_____

_____

_____

_____

DAY 342

Hard work is healthy. It is a part of God's plan for us all. The only place success comes before work is in the dictionary.

"If a man will not work, he shall not eat."
2 Thessalonians 3:10 NIV

PRAYER LIST	TO DO LIST
1. _____	1. _____
2. _____	2. _____
3. _____	3. _____
4. _____	4. _____
5. _____	5. _____
6. _____	6. _____
7. _____	7. _____

Prayer journal notes:

Daniel 8-10; III John

_____
_____
_____
_____
_____
_____
_____
_____
_____
_____

DAY 343

There is no giant that you will face today that is bigger than your God.

"He determines the number of the stars and calls them each by name. Great is our Lord and mighty in power."
Psalm 147:5-6 NIV

PRAYER LIST	TO DO LIST
1. _____	1. _____
2. _____	2. _____
3. _____	3. _____
4. _____	4. _____
5. _____	5. _____
6. _____	6. _____
7. _____	7. _____

Prayer journal notes:

Daniel 11-12; Jude

_____

_____

_____

_____

_____

_____

_____

_____

_____

DAY 344

◦◦◦

If technology continues to improve, maybe one day it will be as fast and as trustworthy as prayer.

"The Lord our God is near us whenever we pray to Him."
Deuteronomy 4:7 NIV

PRAYER LIST	TO DO LIST
1. _____	1. _____
2. _____	2. _____
3. _____	3. _____
4. _____	4. _____
5. _____	5. _____
6. _____	6. _____
7. _____	7. _____

Prayer journal notes:

Hosea 1-4; Revelation 1

_____

_____

_____

_____

_____

_____

_____

_____

_____

_____

DAY 345

The best gift you can give to anyone is a gift of yourself; a visit, a hug, a meal, a word of encouragement, a deed of kindness.

"I do not want to see you now and make only a passing visit; I hope to spend some time with you."

1 Corinthians 16:7 NIV

PRAYER LIST	TO DO LIST
1. _____	1. _____
2. _____	2. _____
3. _____	3. _____
4. _____	4. _____
5. _____	5. _____
6. _____	6. _____
7. _____	7. _____

Prayer journal notes:

Hosea 5-8; Revelation 2

_____

_____

_____

_____

_____

_____

_____

DAY 346

We are often too nonchalant in our worship. Lest we forget Who we are worshipping?

> *"For the Lord is the great God, the great King above all gods. In His hand are the depths of the earth, and the mountain peaks belong to Him. The sea is His for He made it, and His hands formed the dry land."*
>
> *Psalm 95:3-5 NIV*

PRAYER LIST	TO DO LIST
1. _____	1. _____
2. _____	2. _____
3. _____	3. _____
4. _____	4. _____
5. _____	5. _____
6. _____	6. _____
7. _____	7. _____

Prayer journal notes:

Hosea 9-11; Revelation 3

_____

_____

_____

_____

_____

_____

_____

_____

DAY 347

There is no better time than quiet time with God, as there is no one better to talk to than the person who loves you the most.

"I call on You, O God, for You will answer me...show the wonder of Your great love...keep me as the apple of Your eye."

Psalm 17:6-8 NIV

PRAYER LIST	TO DO LIST
1. _____	1. _____
2. _____	2. _____
3. _____	3. _____
4. _____	4. _____
5. _____	5. _____
6. _____	6. _____
7. _____	7. _____

Prayer journal notes:

Hosea 12-14; Revelation 4

_____

_____

_____

_____

_____

_____

_____

_____

DAY 348

If you have a warm bed, a roof over your head, and clean running water, you are better off than millions of people around the world. May our hearts be broken by the things that break the heart of God.

> *"For the Lord searches every heart and understands every motive."*
>
> 1 Chronicles 28:9 NIV

PRAYER LIST	TO DO LIST
1. _____	1. _____
2. _____	2. _____
3. _____	3. _____
4. _____	4. _____
5. _____	5. _____
6. _____	6. _____
7. _____	7. _____

Prayer journal notes:

Joel; Revelation 5

_____
_____
_____
_____
_____
_____
_____
_____

DAY 349

Things will happen that we do not understand, that break our heart, that devastate our lives. We may even get angry with God. Even so, we should still turn to Him. Every other option is temporary. He is eternal.

> *"Lord, to whom shall we go? You have the words of eternal life."*
>
> *John 6:6 NIV*

PRAYER LIST	TO DO LIST
1. _____	1. _____
2. _____	2. _____
3. _____	3. _____
4. _____	4. _____
5. _____	5. _____
6. _____	6. _____
7. _____	7. _____

Prayer journal notes:

Amos 1-3; Revelation 6

_____
_____
_____
_____
_____
_____
_____
_____

DAY 350

Our forgiveness is a done deal. Jesus made sure of that on the cross.

"He forgave us all our sins…He took them away, nailing them to the cross."

Colossians 2:13-14 NIV

PRAYER LIST	TO DO LIST
1. _____	1. _____
2. _____	2. _____
3. _____	3. _____
4. _____	4. _____
5. _____	5. _____
6. _____	6. _____
7. _____	7. _____

Prayer journal notes:

Amos 4-6; Revelation 7

_____

_____

_____

_____

_____

_____

_____

_____

_____

DAY 351

Any time we leave our anger unchecked, we are asking for trouble. Let it go. Give it to God.

> *"In your anger do not sin. Do not let the sun go down while you are still angry, and do not give the devil a foothold."*
>
> *Ephesians 4:26-27 NIV*

PRAYER LIST	TO DO LIST
1. _____	1. _____
2. _____	2. _____
3. _____	3. _____
4. _____	4. _____
5. _____	5. _____
6. _____	6. _____
7. _____	7. _____

Prayer journal notes:

Amos 7-9; Revelation 8

_____

_____

_____

_____

_____

_____

_____

DAY 352

Our faith in God should make a noticeable difference. It should change and dictate everything in our lives.

"We were therefore buried with Him through a new baptism into death in order that, just as Christ was raised from the dead...we too may live a new life."
Romans 6:4 NIV

PRAYER LIST	TO DO LIST
1. _____	1. _____
2. _____	2. _____
3. _____	3. _____
4. _____	4. _____
5. _____	5. _____
6. _____	6. _____
7. _____	7. _____

Prayer journal notes:

Obadiah; Revelation 9

_____

_____

_____

_____

_____

_____

_____

_____

DAY 353

There are times in life when we want to just run away. If you decide to run, remember where to run.

"The name of the Lord is a strong tower; the righteous run to it and are safe."

Proverbs 18:10 NIV

PRAYER LIST	TO DO LIST
1. _____	1. _____
2. _____	2. _____
3. _____	3. _____
4. _____	4. _____
5. _____	5. _____
6. _____	6. _____
7. _____	7. _____

Prayer journal notes:

Jonah; Revelation 10

_____

_____

_____

_____

_____

_____

_____

_____

_____

DAY 354

Throughout history we have come to realize that God has all the answers. We just need to make sure we go to Him with all of our questions.

> *"Call to Me and I will answer you and tell you great and unsearchable things you do not know."*
>
> *Jeremiah 33:3 NIV*

PRAYER LIST	TO DO LIST
1. _____	1. _____
2. _____	2. _____
3. _____	3. _____
4. _____	4. _____
5. _____	5. _____
6. _____	6. _____
7. _____	7. _____

Prayer journal notes:

Micah 1-3; Revelation 11

_____

_____

_____

_____

_____

_____

_____

_____

DAY 355

Don't be a procrastinator. You are always better and have less chance for error when not in a hurry.

> *"The plans of the diligent lead to profit as surely as haste leads to poverty."*
>
> Proverbs 21:5 NIV

PRAYER LIST	TO DO LIST
1. _____	1. _____
2. _____	2. _____
3. _____	3. _____
4. _____	4. _____
5. _____	5. _____
6. _____	6. _____
7. _____	7. _____

Prayer journal notes:

Micah 4-5; Revelation 12

_____

_____

_____

_____

_____

_____

_____

_____

_____

DAY 356

⌒♾⌒

Don't be content to wait and see what will happen if you can take action to make the right thing happen.

"As iron sharpens iron, so one man sharpens another."
Proverbs 27:17 NIV

PRAYER LIST	TO DO LIST
1. _____	1. _____
2. _____	2. _____
3. _____	3. _____
4. _____	4. _____
5. _____	5. _____
6. _____	6. _____
7. _____	7. _____

Prayer journal notes:

Micah 6-7; Revelation 13

_____

_____

_____

_____

_____

_____

_____

_____

_____

_____

DAY 357

Obstacles happen for a reason. Sometimes God wants you to learn from being in the wilderness before He leads you to the promised land.

"...so that you may have the strength to go in and take over the land that you are crossing the Jordan to possess."
Deuteronomy 11:18 NIV

PRAYER LIST	TO DO LIST
1. _____	1. _____
2. _____	2. _____
3. _____	3. _____
4. _____	4. _____
5. _____	5. _____
6. _____	6. _____
7. _____	7. _____

Prayer journal notes:

Nahum; Revelation 14

_____

_____

_____

_____

_____

_____

_____

_____

DAY 358

There is wisdom in looking at the bright side of life. Not just that the glass is half full, but is refillable.

"Make me hear joy and gladness."

Psalm 51:8 NKJV

PRAYER LIST	TO DO LIST
1. _____	1. _____
2. _____	2. _____
3. _____	3. _____
4. _____	4. _____
5. _____	5. _____
6. _____	6. _____
7. _____	7. _____

Prayer journal notes:

Habakkuk; Revelation 15

_____

_____

_____

_____

_____

_____

_____

_____

_____

_____

_____

DAY 359

God gives us hope, not by always changing our circumstances, but by changing us and how we deal with our circumstances.

> *"Now may the God of hope fill you with all joy and peace in believing, that you may abound in hope by the power of the Holy Spirit."*
>
> Romans 15;13 NKJV

PRAYER LIST	TO DO LIST
1. _____	1. _____
2. _____	2. _____
3. _____	3. _____
4. _____	4. _____
5. _____	5. _____
6. _____	6. _____
7. _____	7. _____

Prayer journal notes:

Zephaniah; Revelation 16

_____
_____
_____
_____
_____
_____
_____
_____

DAY 360

The world is interested in knowing how many people work for you. Jesus is interested in knowing how many people you work for.

"I am among you as One who serves."

Luke 22:27 NIV

PRAYER LIST	TO DO LIST
1. _____	1. _____
2. _____	2. _____
3. _____	3. _____
4. _____	4. _____
5. _____	5. _____
6. _____	6. _____
7. _____	7. _____

Prayer journal notes:

Haggai; Revelation 17

_____

_____

_____

_____

_____

_____

_____

_____

_____

DAY 361

Why do we ever think we need a backup plan? There is never a day when Jesus is not the way.

"Do you think I cannot call on my Father, and He will at once put at My disposal more than twelve legions of angels?...I am the way, the truth, and the life."
Matthew 26:53, John 14:6 NIV

PRAYER LIST	TO DO LIST
1. _____	1. _____
2. _____	2. _____
3. _____	3. _____
4. _____	4. _____
5. _____	5. _____
6. _____	6. _____
7. _____	7. _____

Prayer journal notes:

Zechariah 1-4; Revelation 18

_____
_____
_____
_____
_____
_____
_____
_____

DAY 362

Be comforted in knowing that this morning, in the boardroom of heaven, the CEO of the universe assigned guardian angels for your protection today.

> *"For He will command His angels concerning you, to guard you in all your ways."*
>
> *Psalm 91:11 NIV*

PRAYER LIST	TO DO LIST
1. _____	1. _____
2. _____	2. _____
3. _____	3. _____
4. _____	4. _____
5. _____	5. _____
6. _____	6. _____
7. _____	7. _____

Prayer journal notes:

Zechariah 5-8; Revelation 19

_____

_____

_____

_____

_____

_____

_____

_____

DAY 363

The unusual is God's standard procedure.
Just ask Abraham.

> *"And so from this one man (Abraham), and he as good
> as dead, came descendants as numerous as the stars in
> the sky."*
>
> Hebrews 11:11-12 NIV

PRAYER LIST	TO DO LIST
1. _____	1. _____
2. _____	2. _____
3. _____	3. _____
4. _____	4. _____
5. _____	5. _____
6. _____	6. _____
7. _____	7. _____

Prayer journal notes:

Zechariah 9-12; Revelation 20

_____
_____
_____
_____
_____
_____
_____
_____

DAY 364

God places difficult people in your life so that you can learn from them how not to act.

> *"Do not be like them, for your Father knows what you need before you ask Him."*
>
> Matthew 6:8 NIV

PRAYER LIST	TO DO LIST
1. _____	1. _____
2. _____	2. _____
3. _____	3. _____
4. _____	4. _____
5. _____	5. _____
6. _____	6. _____
7. _____	7. _____

Prayer journal notes:

Zechariah 13-14; Revelation 21

_____

_____

_____

_____

_____

_____

_____

_____

_____

DAY 365

Let us praise God for all the blessings of this past year, but also for the troubles and trials that have caused us to grow closer to Him.

"For great is the Lord and most worthy of praise."
1 Chronicles 16:25 NIV

PRAYER LIST	TO DO LIST
1. _____	1. _____
2. _____	2. _____
3. _____	3. _____
4. _____	4. _____
5. _____	5. _____
6. _____	6. _____
7. _____	7. _____

Prayer journal notes:

Malachi; Revelation 22

_____

_____

_____

_____

_____

_____

_____

_____

Volume 1, 2020
Rev. Dr. Joey Edwards
Arlington TN

It is my prayer that God has spoken to you through many of these devotions, that you have grown closer to Him through daily quiet time and the compiling of your prayer journal, and that you have been able to read through the Bible in 365 days (or more). Please share your praises and blessings with me at ***edwardsjoey@bellsouth.net***.

Volume 1, 2020   Day 1- Day 365
Volume 2, 2021   January 1 – December 31

ABOUT THE AUTHOR

Reverend Dr. Joey Edwards has been serving in ministry for 30 years. As an ordained Cumberland Presbyterian minister, he has served as pastor for several churches in the West Tennessee area. He has also served as a college professor for the past 12 years, teaching in the areas of Business and Religion. The daily "Inspirational Thought" has been a part of his ministry since 2008, and goes out daily to congregants, former students, classmates, friends and family throughout the country. His educational background includes a B.S. in Business and MBA from the University of Tennessee at Martin, and a MDiv and DMin from Memphis Theological Seminary.

Printed in the United States
By Bookmasters